A
SENSE
OF
BELONGING

A
SENSE
OF
BELONGING

Norman Bales

20th Century Christian Foundation
2809 12th Avenue South
Nashville, TN 37204

ISBN 0-89098-097-7

Dedication

To

Della Pack

who thought she saw a potential writer in the West Texas farm boy who enrolled in her freshman English class, and who showed him how to go beyond the construction of simple declaratory sentences;

And to

Mima Ann Williams

who loved the English language enough to insist that it should be spoken and written correctly; and who persistently badgered this student to the point that he determined to do his very best when he tried to write down his thoughts on paper.

CONTENTS

CONTENTS

Foreword

God rescues through relationships. He put on flesh and came among us. From the rich vein of this golden truth Norman Bales has mined a treasure of timely help for churches serious about rescuing alienated wanderers.

There is no magic to keeping members healthy, growing and vitally involved in the life of the church. God's design simply calls for genuine relationships! Meaningful relationships, however, are costly. They are not only time-consuming but emotionally draining. Perhaps this painful reality may explain the tendency of churches to replace the fruitful art of "people-sensitive" service with manipulative tactics wrapped in slick packaging. But these easy solutions which appear promising in the short run ultimately prove disastrous.

As we learn to see people as God sees people we will not so easily fall prey to hucksters peddling cheap patches for the church's back-door leakage problem. Quick fixes and impersonal programs have, in many cases, done more to isolate than to woo the wandering one.

Our kind of world extends little warmth to those it deems "different." To relate with other cultures, values, and beliefs invites too many complications for the average self-sick North American. This disease has infected the church to epidemic proportions. Often our most well-intentioned efforts betray our ethnocentric and religiocentric insensitivity. While we verbalize a welcome to all comers, invisible signs declare, "you won't be welcome here unless you look like us." Wrapped up inside the sub-culture of church life, we easily become blind to the perspectives of the outsider. He may desperately want to be an "insider." We may genuinely want him. But we may inadvertently be flashing him the wrong signals.

Helpful steps suggested in this volume are long overdue. They could carry the church a long day's journey toward genuinely redemptive fellowship. Norman Bales pin-points a number of simple and practical things churches can do to engage alienated and unchurched believers. While his book is intensely practical it is by no means shallow. His thoughtful insights are both theologically astute and scripturally sound.

Throughout the volume, one note consistently sounds: We must treat people as God treats people, or all the well-oiled programs we may contrive will not off-set our insensitivity.

Read on and be blessed.

Lynn Anderson
Abilene, Texas

Preface

In the twenty-eight years I have served the church as a full-time minister of the gospel, I've been frustrated by our losses. I think back to the many good people whom I've helped to enter the kingdom, only to see them become inactive and ultimately withdraw from all participation in the fellowship of the church. To me, this has been a disappointment that has marred an otherwise satisfying ministry.

About four years ago, I sat down in earnest to discover better ways of helping new members develop a sense of belonging. My eyes were first opened to the social dynamics of assimilation when I attended a church growth workshop conducted by Win and Charles Arn in 1981 in Minneapolis. Win Arn is the executive director of the American Institute for Church Growth, based in Pasadena, California. The organization researches the dynamics of church growth across a wide spectrum of religious commitments. The sociological research conducted by the leaders of a philosophy which has come to be called "church growth thinking," provides significant insights into the relationship patterns that one encounters in the Churches of Christ. Most of these insights are biblically based and scientifically verifiable. Since that time I've read everything I could get my hands on that concerns incorporating new members.

I first shared some of the information that I had developed with the Central Church of Christ in Cedar Rapids, Iowa, in 1982. Shortly thereafter, I conducted a series of workshops among some of the Iowa churches. The give and take during discussion periods and informal conversation during break times helped sensitize me to the problems both of new members in finding acceptance and of older members in knowing how to extend it. In the spring of 1985, the workshop was given at the LaVega church in Waco, Texas. Conducting the workshop away from the Midwest confirmed my belief that the dynamics involved in helping new members adapt to their new church home isn't confined to any one geographical region.

Some of the material presented in this book appeared serially in the *Christian Bible Teacher* during 1981 and 1982.

I would like to thank Dr. Joe Schubert of the Center for Church Growth in Houston, Texas, who read the first two chapters of the manuscript and encouraged me to complete the writing of the book. Joe Schubert, former minister at the Bammel Road Church of Christ in Houston, Texas, has rendered a great service to our brotherhood in helping us understand how "church growth thinking" relates to our fellowship. I'm also indebted to Lynn Anderson of the Highland church in Abilene, Texas, for recommending the Win Arn workshop to me and for his insights concerning the nature of a Palestinian shepherd's work and its application to relationship building. A much fuller presentation of Lynn's views on relationships is contained in the tape series *Jesus and People,* which may be ordered from the Highland church. I'm also indebted to Dr. Bob Rigdon of Western Carolina University in Cullowhee, North Carolina, for his perceptions of emotional needs. I've attempted to adapt his thoughts to the needs of new Christians.

The basic thesis of this book insists that we can only be successful in helping new Christians develop a sense of belonging as we give priority to forming and maintaining caring relationships. In the past our approach to maturing new converts has been primarily information-centered. I'm not advocating abandonment of information. As a matter of fact, one entire chapter is devoted to the information needs of the new Christian. Even so, the inadequacy of information alone is pretty much summed up in the statement, "People don't care how much we know until they know how much we care."

I want to express my thanks to Ann Quentin, Central's church secretary who typed, printed, stapled, and folded materials used in the workshops. She also typed the first articles I wrote on the subject. She has faithfully and systematically filed the data I've been collecting for the past four years. This book could never have gotten off the ground without her.

I want to express appreciation to Dr. and Mrs. John Borkowski of Sturgis, Michigan, who provided use of their lake cottage so that I could go into hibernation and bring this manuscript to completion. I also wish to thank Don and Gayle Horton of Atlanta, Georgia for making arrangements for me to use the cottage.

Last but not least, I want to thank my wife, Ann, for her faithful support over the past twenty-five years, for believing in my abilities as a writer, and for proofreading the manuscript and patiently enduring my objections when she said, "But, Honey, wouldn't this sound better?" And I would like to thank my children, Elliott, Jim, Ruby, and Gary, whose basic attitude toward my plans for the book could be summed up in the words, "Go for it, Dad."

Norman L. Bales
Sturgis, Michigan
September 20, 1985

Biographical Sketch of the Author

Norman Bales is a graduate of Abilene Christian University. He has preached for the Central Church of Christ in Cedar Rapids, Iowa, since 1977.

Chapter One

Measuring Evangelistic Success

Churches in the Restoration Movement frequently measure church growth by the number of people they baptize. Growth reports in brotherhood journals consistently emphasize baptisms. A publication circulated among our brethren recently reported a church growth story under the headline "How _____ (name of congregation) Baptized 110." Church leaders often measure the effectiveness of their ministries by the ability of any given ministry to produce baptisms. Periodicals regularly publish the names of congregations who succeed in baptizing more than 100 people in a calendar year. Preachers who serve those churches find themselves being asked to appear on lecture programs and workshops to tell how they did it.

Looking Beyond Baptism

Without question baptism does and should figure prominently in any attempt to gauge evangelistic progress. Paul describes a new life which begins at baptism in Romans 6:3-4. The fact remains, however, that baptism represents only the beginning and not the completion of the new life. The church must take the initiative to urge its baptized members to "attain the unity of the faith and the knowledge of the Son of God to mature manhood to the measure of the stature of the fullness of Christ" (Ephesians 4:13). We must be concerned about what happens to believers six months, one year, or five years after baptism.

Evidence From Recent Studies

Church growth reports are not so sensational when we measure growth by those who stay in the church year after year. Many churches don't even bother to keep statistics designed to monitor the growth of new Christians. If they did, they might be shocked to discover a rather high attrition rate among new Christians.

From 1965 to 1980, almanacs and yearbooks listed the numerical strength of the churches of Christ at about 3,000,000. The figure was actually an educated guess supplied by leaders within our brotherhood. Its accuracy has always been suspect. In 1979, Mac Lynn of the Harding Graduate School in Memphis, Tennessee, undertook a county-by-county survey in an attempt to discover the true numerical strength of congregations in the United States. He discovered only 1,244,094 members, which is considerably less than the 3,000,000 figure previously reported.[1]

Flavil R. Yeakley, Jr., a social scientist and student of church growth patterns, offers the following explanation for the disparity of figures:

> The total population of the United States according to the 1980 federal census is over 225,000,000. Religious census data on many local communities indicate that there are more members of the church of Christ who are not identified with any local congregation than the total number of all those who are identified with all congregations of the church of Christ. If this condition prevails nationwide, it

2

is possible that there are 2,000,000 to 3,000,000 people who would say they are members of the church of Christ if anyone ever asked them. But the church of Christ cannot count on these non-identified members.[2]

Yeakley's assessment of the situation at least suggests the possibility that we may be losing about half of those whom we convert. As a matter of fact, Yeakley goes on to suggest that the high dropout rate significantly alters the growth patterns of the typical church.

In a typical church there are around 160 members and only eight baptisms per year. Six children of church members and two other people who are baptized each year in that typical congregation. Half of these eventually drop out of the church. The typical congregation is baptizing only four permanent converts per year. When the average annual death rate is subtracted that leaves a net annual growth rate of less than one percent.[3]

These surveys point out the need to correct the current trend. Some would suggest that the church needs to intensify its evangelistic outreach and baptize more people. Indeed, the church does need to baptize more people. Those churches baptizing more than a hundred people each year are setting a pace that more of us need to follow. Even so, baptizing more people is really counterproductive if we are going to continue to lose half of those whom we baptize. The number of baptisms may increase, but if we are also losing more people, then how do we account to God for an increase in losses?

There's a temptation to relax our concern when we can see more people walking through our front doors than we notice leaving our fellowship through the back door. If Christians fall into the habit of concerning themselves only with the arithmetic of church growth, they may well find themselves reacting insensitively to the worth of human souls. Any time a person chooses to disassociate himself from participation in the life of the church, we ought to be concerned about the motives behind such a negative decision. Our respect for individual personhood demands that we concentrate on ways of intensifying our efforts to retain newly baptized converts in active participation.

In the early seventies, the church growth movement began to make its influence felt across a broad spectrum of American church life. Donald McGavran, who is generally thought of as the father of the church growth movement, and those associated with him revolutionized foreign missions through the application of scientific principles of growth to missionary enterprises. In the early seventies attention was turned toward the application of these same principles to the growth of American churches. In the churches where these principles have been understood and practiced, remarkable growth has taken place.

A keystone principle in the church growth movement is the incorporation of new members into active church life. C. Peter Wagner, associate professor of church growth at Fuller Theological Seminary in Pasadena, California, writes, "...if a person does not eventually make a commitment to the body of Christ...there is little reason to suppose that a disciple has been made."[4] Lyle E. Schaller of the Yokefellow Institute in Richmond, Indiana, claims that "it is unChristian for a congregation to seek new members unless it is willing and able to accept them into that called out community."[5] Win Arn, executive director of the American Institute for American Church Growth, says, "Evangelism is not complete without the new Christians becoming an active part of the church."[6]

The evidence from all these sources points to one overpowering conclusion. Churches must work diligently to assist new members, who have been invited to become a part of our fellowship, to become productive members. From a church growth standpoint, we cannot afford to lose half of those whom we win. Furthermore, we owe a debt to the

4

people we bring to Christ. They deserve to be assisted in becoming mature disciples of Christ. Neglect is inexcusable. Abandonment is criminal. We must never forget the language of Peter: "For if, after they have escaped the defilements of the world through the knowledge of our Lord and Savior Jesus Christ, they are again entangled in them and overpowered, the last state has become worse for them than the first" (2 Peter 2:20).

Definition of Terms

In this study, two terms will be used to describe the process of helping new members (and maybe even some old ones) to feel they belong. The first word is *incorporation*. Incorporation, as we are using the term in this study, means to combine or mix together. When a homemaker bakes a cake, she uses several different ingredients. In today's world of prepackaged foods, she will probably start with a cake mix.

To this she will likely add milk, eggs, and vegetable oil. She stirs these ingredients until the milk, eggs, and vegetable oil become thoroughly incorporated with the cake mix. Once the mixing is completed, the ingredients become inseparable. As Christians we must decide if we are willing to mix new members in so thoroughly with older members that a similar inseparable blend of personalities takes place.

The other term is *assimilation*, which means the process of absorption. All of us consume food at regular intervals. The digestive system breaks down the food into body chemicals which in turn become assimilated into the body system. This assimilation process keeps the body alive. The New Testament compares the church to a human body in Ephesians 1:22-23 and in other passages. Many comparisons are made throughout scripture between the way the human body functions and the way the church body functions. Paul touches on the assimilation idea in 1 Corinthians 12:26 when he says, "If one member suffers all suffer together; if one is honored, all rejoice together." The assimilation idea suggests an intrinsic bonding of the various members of the church in the lives of one another. We cannot keep new Christians at arm's length and expect assimilation to occur.

Incorporation in the Great Commission

Incorporation is inherent in the command to evangelize. According to Matthew's account of the Great Commission, Jesus entrusted the apostles to "go therefore and make disciples of all nations, baptizing them in the name of the Father and of the Son and of the Holy Spirit, teaching them to observe all that I have commanded you and lo, I am with you always to the close of the age" (Matthew 28:19-20). The emphasis of the commission is on making disciples. The process of disciple making begins prior to baptism and continues after baptism. If the teaching, the caring, and the loving stops at baptism, it is clear that the disciple maker has stopped short of completing his responsibility toward the one who is in the process of becoming a disciple.

Surely the apostles understood that the command to make disciples included the incorporation process. Jesus recruited twelve men from diverse backgrounds. Some of them came from a fishing background (Andrew, Peter, James, and John). One was a tax collector (Matthew) and still another was a known political activist (Simon the zealot). The latter two well may have been on opposite ends of the first-century political spectrum. This very select cadre of men whom Jesus elected to serve in the vanguard of his worldwide mission to appeal to the deepest needs of people consisted of a group of individuals with diverse temperaments, abilities, and biases. Even so, Jesus managed to mold eleven of these men into a cohesive force that eventually influenced life in every corner of the globe. He incorporated them into his mission by putting his life down by the side of their lives. He gave freely of his time and energy to build their faith When he left the earth at the end of a three-year ministry, he left with the confidence that the goal of world evangelism would be achieved. As they heard him describe the discipling process, they knew exactly what he meant. After all, they had observed his example. They had become assimilated into fellowship with him and with one another, and they would naturally expect to incorporate any newly won converts into their fellowship.

Incorporation in the Early Church

Charles Shaver writes, "There are at least 32 follow-up instances and 18 other occasions in Acts where the concept of encouragement is displayed."[7] I'm not sure I can identify all 32 instances Shaver has in mind, but the Book of Acts does repeatedly emphasize the principle of incorporation.

After Pentecost, new members of the Jerusalem church were made to feel included through instructional opportunity, through personal interaction with one another in daily living, through corporate worshiping, and through participation in the devotional life of the body (Acts 2:42-47). The apostles devoted themselves to providing the informational needs of those who were newly baptized. A spirit of mutual sharing developed within the fellowship to such a high degree that "all who believed were together and had all things in common" (Acts 2:44). Homes were opened wide to other Christians and food was shared together on a daily basis. The extent of their incorporation is indicated by the comment that the members of the newly formed church were "praising God and having favor with all the people and the Lord added to their number day by day those who were being saved" (Acts 2:46-47).

Saul's entrance into the fellowship provides some interesting insights into the incorporation process. The church in Jerusalem was really quite hesitant to incorporate this fellow who had created so much trouble for the church. Fortunately Saul found a sensitive person named Barnabas who was willing to risk his own reputation in the church in order to assimilate Saul into the fellowship. "But Barnabas took him and brought him to the apostles and declared to them how on the road he had seen the Lord, who spoke to him and how at Damascus he preached boldly in his name" (Acts 9:27).

Later, the church in Jerusalem sent Barnabas to Antioch to help stabilize the gains being made by the church in its ministry to the Greeks. Saul was still in Tarsus. His active preaching ministry really had not gotten off the ground. Barnabas went looking for Saul, "and when he had found him, he brought him to Antioch. For a whole year they met with the church and taught a large company of people" (Acts 11:26). When Barnabas developed an interest in Saul's incorporation, his latent talent as a teacher and preacher of the Word began to emerge. We remember Saul for his phenomenal missionary energy as a church planter, but we also need to remember that his preaching really began because Barnabas was sensitive to the need of incorporation.

In Acts 20, we have a record of Paul's meeting with the elders of the church in Ephesus in which he recalled the highlights of his ministry with the Ephesian church. In verse 20 he says, "I did not shrink from declaring anything that was profitable and teaching you in public and from house to house." The context would indicate that Paul's house-to-house work was done as a means of stabilizing Christians. The intensity of his incorporation was such that he says in verse 31, "Therefore be alert, remembering that for three years I did not cease night or day to admonish everyone with tears."

Incorporation Problems in the Early Church

Incorporation was not always a smooth process in the early church. Then, as now, some people were difficult to assimilate. Then, as now, church members found it necessary to break their comfortable relationship patterns in order to make the church incorporation-conscious.

After getting such a marvelous start in the incorporation of new members, the Jerusalem church struck an incorporation snag by neglecting ministry to one particular class of women. "Now in these days when the disciples were increasing in number, the Hellenists murmured against the Hebrews because their widows were being neglected in the daily distribution" (Acts 6:2). The Hellenists comprised a homogeneous subgrouping among the members of the Jerusalem church. Somehow their assimilation into the group that had all things in common just didn't take place.

The apostles had their hands full teaching and praying. It didn't seem right to abandon that kind of work, so they asked the church to select men who then in turn were assigned the task of taking care of the Hellenistic widows. These men were given roles to fulfill in which they were required to exercise responsible, compassionate judgment. As a result, verse 5 says, "And what they said pleased the whole multitude." Few problems are ever settled so quickly and so neatly, but the key to the solution lies in the fact that the apostles first recognized that an incorporation problem existed and then they acted to bring about a happy solution.

Another incorporation problem is reported in Galatians 2. Again, a homogeneous subgroup in the church was not being assimilated. This time, Jewish Christians were discriminating against Gentile Christians. A group of outside agitators had created a conflict between those who belonged to different cultural and ethnic groups. Peter had aligned himself with the group which conformed to the cultural patterns in which he had been reared—Judaism. He pulled away from the group that practiced different cultural habits—the Gentiles. He refused to eat meals with them, even though he had done so prior to the arrival of the agitators from Jerusalem. In the mind of Paul, this was inconsistent behavior. So Paul writes, "When Cephas came to Antioch, I opposed him to his face because he stood condemned" (Galatians 2:11). Again, an incorporation crisis was averted because Paul recognized the fact that an incorporation problem existed and was even willing to risk direct confrontation with a fellow apostle in order to promote assimilation.

Our Need for Incorporation

The Scriptures harmonize with the conclusion of the modern students of church growth concerning incorporation. Evangelism does not end with conversion. Incorporation is a part of the process of evangelizing. In helping new Christians become absorbed into the life of the church, we need to exhibit the same kind of interest that we display toward getting people into our baptistries.

When we measure church growth solely by the number of baptisms we record in any given year, our measurement gauge is faulty. Win Arn bluntly challenges our measuring standards when he says,

> Let's measure success six months to five years later (after conversion), when that person is incorporated into the body of Christ and living as a disciple should live in the fellowship with Christ, a reasonable part of the local church and walking as a Christian should walk in the world.[8]

Questions for Discussion

1. Why do church leaders in the Restoration Movement tend to focus on baptism as the primary gauge for determining evangelistic success?
2. How can we curb the tendency to relax our concern when our gains exceed our losses?
3. Why do leaders in the church growth movement place such a high priority on the incorporation of new members?
4. What steps has the church taken in the past to see that its members are fully assimilated into the body?
5. Which of these has been effective? ineffective? Why?
6. Since the incorporation principles are so obviously taught in scripture, why are they often neglected in the church?
7. What can we learn about incorporation from the relationship between Jesus and the apostles?
8. What evidence of incorporation consciousness do we discover in the Book of Acts?
9. How can the apostles' sensitive response to the neglect of the Grecian widows help us become more successful in assimilating members today?
10. What can be done to raise the level of incorporation awareness in the congregation where you worship?

Endnotes

[1]Mac Lynn, *Where the Saints Meet* (Austin, Texas: Firm Foundation Publishing House, 1982), p. ix. Since this manuscript was initially prepared, Dr. Lynn has updated these figures. In 1987 he reports 1,275,533 members in the United States, excluding territories.

[2]Flavil R. Yeakley, Jr., *Why Churches Grow,* 3rd ed. (Arvada, Colorado: Christian Communications, Inc., 1979), p. v.

[3]*Ibid.*, p. 1.

[4]C. Peter Wagner, *Your Church Can Grow* (Glendale, California: Regal Publications, 1976), p. 137.

[5]Lyle E. Schaller, *Assimilating New Members* (Nashville, Tennessee: Abingdon Press, 1978), p. 128.

[6]Win and Charles Arn, *The Master's Plan for Making Disciples* (Pasadena, California: Church Growth Press, 1982), p. 143.

[7]Charles Shaver, "The Morning After," in *How to Effectively Incorporate New Members, ed. Win and Charles Arn.* (Pasadena, California: American Institute for Church Growth, 1981), p. 64.

[8]Win Arn, ed., *The Pastor's Church Growth Handbook* (Pasaadena, California: Church Growth Press, 1979), p. 47.

Chapter Two

Why Do We Lose So Many New Members?

The birth experience ranks as one of life's most exciting moments. Prospective parents most often devote themselves completely to making plans for the new arrival. They designate a special room of the house to be the nursery. Their shopping interests undergo radical changes. They begin acquiring bassinets, baby beds, playpens, diaper bags, rattles, bottles, and sterilizers. They make extensive plans to nurture a new child once he makes his entry into the world.

When the blessed event takes place, the new father quickly telephones relatives, friends, and acquaintances. He seemingly spares no expense to share the good news with everyone who is close to him. Handshakes, hugs, and congratulatory messages are the order of the day. The parents want everyone else to know about the joyful event, so they send out birth announcements revealing the child's name, weight, and length. A spirit of celebration engulfs the new parents' entire friendship circle.

New spiritual life can also be quite exciting. Some of the happiest moments in the life of a church take place when a small group of people gather around some person who has made the decision to let Jesus rule in his life. While preparations for baptism are being made, those who have gathered to witness this pivotal event enthusiastically offer hymns of praise and gratitude. Heads are reverently bowed while the baptismal candidate is gently lowered beneath the surface of the water, and the strains of "O Happy Day" burst forth from the lips of rejoicing Christians as the new child of God emerges from the water to anticipate a new life of hope and joy. Fervent prayers are offered in behalf of a precious soul who "once was lost but now is found." Tears stream from the eyes of evangelistically concerned Christians who patiently taught the Word of God to this sincere truth seeker. As the new Christian leaves the dressing room to greet his new brothers and sisters in Christ, smiling faces welcome him into the fellowship of the church as arms reach out to embrace him. One of the most beautiful moments in the life of any New Testament church takes place in front of the baptistry because baptism represents the delivery room of rebirth.

Wouldn't it be nice to be able to guarantee a new Christian that he will always experience the same kind of caring and attention that he receives when he is baptized? It would be nice, but can we honestly offer him that assurance? Will he receive the nurture and tender loving care that he needs in order to continue the process of discipleship?

In the case of physical life, the new member of a family usually becomes the center of attention for the other members of the family. Gifts are frequently sent to the family home to assist the parents in postnatal care. Records of his first trip to church, his first visit to the grandparents, and his first experience at the barbershop are all carefully noted in his baby book. Pictures are taken and passed around to anyone who will stop and look at them. For several weeks the spirit of celebration continues.

No one expects an infant to survive on his own resources when he first comes into the world. His diet has to be carefully controlled. He will eventually graduate from his mother's milk (or perhaps formula) to strained baby food and finally to a regular diet. In the first year or two, the clothing worn by an infant is especially designed for quick removal in case he has "an accident." A wholesome diet, simple exercise, and constant encouragement from parents contribute to a remarkable degree of growth in a very short period of time. Clothing has to be discarded before it has worn out because the body is growing so rapidly.

Mental and social growth is also taking place. At play the child learns to interact with other children. He may be taken from his mother's side after about four years and enrolled in a nursery school. Then he goes to kindergarten, where he studies for half a day, and finally he enrolls in the first grade, where he must stay at school all day. Behavior expectations begin to change. At six months, oatmeal on his face may be cute, but at sixteen years, the child is expected to know how to use a napkin.

We usually see the parallel between physical birth and spiritual birth when a person comes into the fellowship of the church. Our terminology even suggests that we are geared to thinking along the lines of the birth analogy. A new Christian is often called "a babe in Christ." In fact, such comparison has support in scripture. When Nicodemus came to Jesus one night, this learned teacher of the law and ruler of the Jews was told, "Truly, truly, I say to you, unless one is born anew, he cannot see the kingdom of God" (John 3:3). Peter urged the exiles of the Dispersion to think in terms of the birth analogy when he said, "Like newborn babes, long for pure spiritual milk that by it, you may grow up into salvation" (1 Peter 2:5).

Developmental Sensitivity

Even with these scriptural precedents to guide us, we don't often apply the same kind of terminology to the developmental stages of the Christian life. In fact, the birth and childhood analogy seems to be dropped shortly after a new Christian's hair gets dry and the strains of "I Have Decided to Follow Jesus" die out. Indifference toward developmental growth can be devastating to the new Christian because a new child of God cannot be incorporated into the body unless more mature Christians recognize developmental needs. Maturing the new Christian includes responding to the new Christian's developmental stage.

1 John 2:12-14 concentrates on at least three developmental stages in the life of a Christian. John says, "I am writing to you little children because your sins are forgiven." The phrase "your sins are forgiven" indicates that he is speaking about spiritual children rather than physical children. "Little children" in this context quite likely refers to the new Christians among John's readers. They haven't learned about all the problems of the church yet, and they haven't developed enough maturity to appreciate the deeper aspects of the Christian message. They simply rejoice in the fact that they have been forgiven of their sins.

The second developmental stage consists of those who are in the fatherhood stage—the mature Christians. The outstanding characteristics of those who have reached this level of maturity is seen in the fact that "they know him who is from the beginning." Over a long period of dedicated service they have acquired an intimate relational knowledge of the Savior. W. E. Vine observes that the word translated "know" in the verse "...indicates a relation between the person knowing and the object known."[1] An intimate bonding has developed between God and those who have reached the fatherhood stage of growth.

In between these two developmental stages, John refers to a group of people whom he classifies as "the young men." They have passed through spiritual infancy, but they have not yet achieved maturity. Three qualities are mentioned concerning this stage of spiritual development: (1) "You have overcome the evil one." They have met the temptations of the flesh and emerged from the contest with Satan victoriously. (2) "You are strong." No longer does every exposure to wickedness and error put them in a defensive position. They have been able to rise above the temptation to be "tossed to and fro and carried about with every wind of doctrine by the cunning of men, by the craftiness of their deceitful lies" (Ephesians 4:14). (3) "The word of God abides in you." The word is more than just a set of law codes. They have internalized the message to the extent that God's will has become the will of the people who have reached this developmental stage. They are, however, still reaching for intimate, relational knowledge of God. Most growing Christians are probably somewhere in this stage. Peter suggests that the knowledge of Christ is not limited when he says, "But grow in grace and knowledge of our Lord and Savior Jesus Christ" (2 Peter 3:18).

Recognizing Developmental Needs

While 1 John 2:12-14 doesn't provide a detailed description of the whole developmental process, the passage does give credence to the thesis that Christians are at different levels of growth. We cannot expect to assimilate new members with effectiveness if we ignore the fact that people at different stages of development have different needs. The specific needs of new Christians will be discussed in later chapters. For now it is important to realize that we must make ourselves incorporation conscious, and we do that by being sensitive to the progress a new Christian makes and by reacting according to the level of growth he has achieved.

Newer Members and Older Members

Because of the developmental process, the member who has recently become a part of a congregation tends to see the church in a totally different light from the member who has been around for several years. The newer member is not aware of strange quirks in the personalities of certain members which the older member takes for granted. The newer member is struggling to get acquainted with many new faces, while the older member already knows most of the people who have been in the fellowship for any length of time. The newer member may come from a totally different culture, family background, and religious orientation. The older member may have roots in the church which reach back for several generations. All these factors have to be considered if incorporation is to become a reality.

A newer member often will become a member of a congregation because he sees that church meeting one or more of his own individual needs. If the new member is single, a singles ministry may be the reason he has decided to cast his lot with a certain church. If the new member is a family-oriented person with small children, that person may be attracted to the fellowship of other young couples who have small children. Some people are attracted to a certain teaching emphasis. Perhaps the new member has been worshiping with a church that denies the inspiration of the Scriptures. He leaves that church in disillusionment to search for a church that believes the Bible. His reason for being there may have something to do with the fact that the Bible is respected and taught. The manner of presentation becomes the determining factor for some people. One person might attend a congregation because the preacher delivers his message with impassioned, arm-waving, pulpit-pounding enthusiasm, while another is attracted to a different congregation because the pulpit presentation is quiet, restrained, and conversational. One person prefers to hear parabolic teaching, while another opts for the didactic method. The attractions vary widely, but most people begin worshiping where they do because they see the church meeting some felt need or desire.

An older member, on the other hand, most likely maintains his membership in the same congregation for a totally different reason. He has been a member long enough to establish some rather deep relationships. Pulpit styles may change over the years, yet he stays. The church may not be doing all that much to respond to any kind of personally felt need, still he wouldn't think of attending somewhere else. After all, his children are married to the children of other members. In fact, he is related to a large number of people within the congregation. He worships where he does because of relationships, not need satisfaction. The problem with relationships as a unifying principle lies in the fact that such relationships tend to become exclusive. No one ever thinks of drawing new members into the relationship pattern. Thus, the same principle which tends to cause an older member to feel he is well incorporated into the church may actually cause a new member to feel left out.

How does one break into a group that is drawn together by existing relationships? How does a person break into a circle of friendship which has developed over a period of several years and has shown no interest in making the friendship circle larger? These are some of the frustrations experienced by any new member when he attempts to become a part of a congregation which is relatively stable in its makeup and passively exclusive in its fellowship practices.

New members tend to be quite enthusiastic about their identification with the church. This is especially true with one who comes into the church as a newly baptized believer. The new Christian is keenly aware that his obedience to Christ has delivered him from the sin which formerly enslaved him (Romans 6:17-18). This new-found freedom energizes the new Christian. He literally glows with a spirit of exhilaration as he describes his new life, his hopes, and his dreams. He wants to learn. He's growing so rapidly that he can see his progress almost daily. He tends to look for and expect the very best behavior from other Christians. He may be oblivious of the shortcomings of Christians at the same time. That doesn't appear to be contradictory in his own mind because he's still sorting out his value system during the first few months of his Christian life. He's also subject to disillusionment. When he learns that other Christians have feet of clay and that they are still struggling after years of church membership, he may well go through a period of discouragement.

While the newer Christian feels relief when the burden of sin has been lifted from his life, the older member may yet be living with another kind of burden. His burden is not the burden of unforgiven sins, but he's burdened by the requirements of the Christian life. Somehow his mind has filtered out the positives, and he's hearing only the negatives. He's told he mustn't drink, smoke, dance, behave lustfully toward the opposite sex, etc. The rigid demands of his religion impose a slavery upon him that becomes burdensome. The joy of salvation has faded from his experience, and he's constantly being reminded from the classroom and from the pulpit that he needs to be more committed to the work of the Lord.

Besides that, he's probably had at least one or more traumatic experiences in the church. The conduct of church leaders may have shaken his confidence in those who profess to be Christians. He may have developed a cynical attitude toward the church in general and toward certain people in the church in particular. He cannot share the enthusiasm of the new Christian because he sees the new Christian's experience as naive optimism and wonders how long it will take for the bubble to burst in the new member's life. He's not doing much to incorporate the new member because he doesn't care all that much about the church anyway. He feels trapped by his church commitments.

The new Christian often feels he's struggling to find his place in the church. If he should be fortunate enough to get an invitation to attend an informal social gathering, he may be disappointed when he attends. Well assimilated church members may be talking about subjects and using terminology beyond the range of his understanding. For example, suppose two ladies who teach pre-school Bible classes decide to invite a third lady who happens to be a new Christian over for coffee some morning. One of the teachers may ask the other, "What did you think of those new take-homes we gave out last Sunday?" The second lady might respond, "I didn't have time to use them. I got involved with handwork and the bell rang before I could distribute them." The new Christian is not oriented to such terms as "take-homes" and "handwork," and hence she feels left out of the conversation. Later on, when she describes the conversation to her husband, she quite likely will report the account of what was said in terms of what "they" said rather than what "we" talked about.

In the early seventies, when environmental issues were prominent, a young conservation activist was converted to Christ. Shortly thereafter he was invited to a fellowship gathering in the church basement. Women of the church served a potluck meal as a gesture of friendship, but they used paper plates, plastic forks and spoons, and styrofoam cups. The young man regarded that kind of tableware to be in violation of his ecological activism. He couldn't understand why a group of people who professed to believe "the earth is the Lord's and the fullness thereof" would be so insensitive as to use kitchen supplies that in his mind had been proven to be environmentally unsound. Of course, the church members had never dreamed that their tableware would be offensive. We must realize that people come to us with a variety of ideas and convictions. It won't do to write such a person off as some kind of "ecological nut." A soul lies in the balance.

Older members already feel a sense of belonging, so they often don't see the need to help someone else feel acceptance. They just assume the new Christian will eventually find his niche. The older member may say, "Well, I remember when I first came here. Nobody helped me find my place in the church. I just had to stick it out, and eventually I came to feel like I belonged." He is too much involved with existing relationships and responsibilities to notice the problems with new Christians.

New Christians are often thinking about things that are going to happen in the future. If the new member hears the leadership talk in terms of future goals and new ministries, he is quite likely to be supportive. He may even envision himself working in one of those new ministries. He's not really concerned about insurmountable objects. No one has told him that it costs too much or that it's impractical or that the opportune moment for such a venture is still in the future. He doesn't know the church tried a certain idea three years ago and it didn't work, nor does he realize the church can't engage in a particular ministry because it has never been done before. He wants to see the church grow, and he wants to be a part of making church growth take place. He believes the greatest years of the church's service to the community lie in the future.

Older members have a tendency to be past-oriented. The fiascoes of the past are firmly embedded in their memories. "I remember when" is a significant part of the vocabulary. Some members probably feel a strong sense of identification with a former minister, and they tend to believe that the church has been going downhill ever since he left. Some older members recall the glory days when they served on building committees and participated in the construction of the church edifice. They are quick to remind a new member, "This building wouldn't be here without the sacrifice of us old timers." When new ideas are suggested, older members often recall the trauma and the conflict that attended new efforts in the past. They complain, "Surely the leadership isn't going to put us through that kind of situation again." They tend to regard the new members as being unrealistically visionary. Church life is mostly in the past not the future.

Because the new members tend to be future-oriented, they usually accept new ideas when they are thrown out. A new member is not an analytical genius who knows seventeen different reasons why a certain ministry idea "simply will not work." He may be short on details, but he's long on enthusiasm, and he's willing to put forth the energy to try to make an idea work. He also may have some problems discriminating between what is proper and what is improper in achieving certain goals. In one congregation, a new Christian was attending his first business meeting. The subject of church finance was the first item on the agenda. The treasurer painted a bleak picture of total financial disaster if contributions did not improve. The new Christian's only previous contact with religion involved a nominal connection with the Roman Catholic church. He asked for permission to speak in the meeting, and when he was recognized, he said, "You guys really ought to think about offering Bingo. There's a lot of money to be made with Bingo. Folks really go for raffles too. We could start having Bingo every Friday night and raffle off some merchandise and take care of our financial problems without any trouble." Of course, the older members of the church were horrified to hear such a suggestion being offered with all seriousness and sincerity. As you might imagine, they quickly took advantage of the situation to teach the new brother the way of the Lord a little more perfectly.

The Maintenance Syndrome

Older members would certainly exercise more caution than the new person who wants to get Bingo going as a means of solving the church's financial crisis, but that very caution can also produce a maintenance mentality. Nearly every creative idea is first viewed either as a threat to the faith or as a potential economic disaster. Older members often want to maintain the status quo. They see little need for altering the way things have been going for the last dozen years or so. Older members have also developed comfortable relationship patterns. They have designed Bible classes to meet their needs and the needs of their children. They don't often think about the need of the new member who comes into the church without any Bible knowledge and brings children who've never been taught how to behave in a Bible class. So when a new member's child speaks a profane expletive in the Bible class, and when he can't go past Exodus in naming the books of the Old Testament, and can't name the builder of the ark, the teacher who has been teaching church members' children all her life may well throw up her hands in exasperation. No one thinks about developing strategies for teaching people who come from unchurched backgrounds. The older members concentrate instead on altering the situations so they only have to teach well scrubbed, polite, reasonably knowledgeable children.

They would prefer those who not only know the names of the books of the Bible but also are able to reel off the names of the kings of Judah and Israel along with the names of the twelve apostles when called on to do so. In short, older members tend to project their concern and their energy toward those who are already a part of the fellowship, with relatively little thought given to the unique problems of those who are new members.

The maintenance syndrome tends to cause Christians to turn their concerns inward instead of outward. The preaching must be what *we* want to hear. The classes must be on what *we* want to study. The work program must be concerned with those areas of ministry that will benefit *us* the most. Effective incorporation cannot take place in a maintenance atmosphere. New members became new members because they were willing to break loose from the status quo. Traditions mean nothing to them, but they do expect to have some of their needs met. The burden of responsibility to help meet those needs lies with older Christians. Paul writes, "We who are strong ought to bear with the failings of the weak and not to please ourselves; let each of us please his neighbor for his good, to edify him" (Romans 15:1-2).

With their enthusiasm for the church and their openness to new ideas, new members provide church leaders with a reservoir of talent which can be deployed in any number of meaningful ministries, but if new Christians are repeatedly ignored, patterns of discontent will inevitably emerge. New Christians may well become disillusioned and lethargic. They will either become passive members or completely recommit their time to some other interest.

It's up to the church to create an atmosphere that ministers to people in all their developmental stages. Church leaders must be sensitive to the developmental process. That sensitivity must filter down to the entire membership. Those who have already found their place in the church must take the initiative to channel the enthusiasm and energy of the new members. No one is suggesting that new Christians be given assignments that are over their heads, but new members must be helped to understand that their ideas are important and their contribution to the work of the Lord is valued. The new Christian is not likely to reach spiritual adulthood under his own power. He needs God's help, but he also needs the help of other Christians. Our responsibility to aid in the incorporation process is perhaps best stated by Paul when he says, "Bear one another's burdens and so fulfill the law of Christ" (Galatians 6:2).

Questions for Discussion

1. Why do we often pay more attention to a person's spiritual birth than to his spiritual growth?
2. Why do we drop the birth and growth analogies soon after a person becomes a Christian?
3. How does 1 John 2:12-14 contribute to our understanding of the developmental process in a Christian's life?
4. What are some of the differences you have noticed between newer members and older members?
5. Why do new members often feel like outsiders?
6. How can we make ourselves more sensitive to the needs and concerns of new members?
7. How can we help older members see the importance of helping new members become incorporated?
8. How can we recognize the maintenance syndrome?
9. How can the maintenance syndrome be reversed?
10. How can we let a new Christian know that he is a valued member of the body?

Endnotes

1W. E. Vine, *Expository Dictionary of New Testament Words* (Old Tappan, New Jersey: Fleming H. Revell Company, 17th Impression, 1966), p. 298.

Chapter Three

What Is
An Incorporated Member?

Not long ago I visited the services of a congregation several hundred miles away from where I live. The church I visited used the same hymnbook and sang the same familiar songs that I knew. The program was quite predictable—a cappella singing, Biblical preaching, prayers, the Lord's Supper, and giving. Those who led the worship employed the same procedures and even much of the same terminology that is used in the service in my home congregation. The song at the end of the sermon is called "the invitation song." The man in the pulpit is not referred to as "the pastor"; rather, he is "the preacher." Both congregations refer to their overseers as "elders," but neither of them ever speaks of "the board." Those who are taken into the fellowship don't "join the church." They "obey the gospel."

A visitor who hasn't been introduced to such unique procedures and terminology might feel out of place in an assembly like this. If a visitor's total worship experience has taken place inside Catholic houses of worship, that person might observe a number of things that appear strange to him. He might well respond negatively to the noisy chat ter which goes on in many churches of Christ prior to the opening of the service. He might even think the members have little respect for the sacredness of the "sanctuary." He doesn't immediately realize that those who are assembled there don't think of it as a sanctuary at all. They prefer to call it an "auditorium." He might also wonder about the artlessness of the building. The architectural design of the assembly place may appear rather drab and plain. He would be puzzled by the absence of statues and other forms of art in the assembly hall. He may find the conducting of the service itself a rather shocking display of informality and lack of attention to any kind of serious liturgy. When he leaves, his response could be, "I don't feel like I've been to church at all."

Consider also the Protestant visitor. His degree of shock may not measure up to that experienced by his Catholic counterpart, but he can be counted on to take note of the absence of instrumental music. He may be wondering, "Are they so poor they can't afford an organ, or do they have something against it?" If he attends repeatedly, he will probably wonder why the Lord's Supper is served every Sunday. Terminology, the lack of formal ritual, and the presence of crying babies in the assembly may well combine to cause him to feel that something is missing in the service.

The unchurched person may have an even greater degree of apprehension. If he shows up at the service dressed in a way that makes him look out of place, he's going to feel quite uncomfortable. He's afraid of saying or doing something that will call attention to himself. He doesn't know what to do when the Lord's Supper is being passed. The a cappella singing may not bother him, but then on the other hand he probably doesn't know the songs. He may be afraid to talk with members afterward, for fear that some of his profane vocabulary might slip out and embarrass him.

Even a visitor from another congregation within our fellowship may not feel totally at ease. While the service itself may be very familiar, the fact remains that the people are strangers. When announcements are made, the visitor pays very little attention to the names of those who are in the hospital. After all, he doesn't have any way of associating a face with the names he's heard from the pulpit.

My home congregation conducts its Sunday morning Bible classes following the general assembly. This practice doesn't violate any scriptural principle, but it does differ from the tradition of many churches of Christ. Sometimes our reversal of the schedule causes visitors to wonder if we are truly sound in the faith. Once in a while an out-of-town visitor notices the times on our sign board and doesn't read them carefully. He decides to skip Bible class and show up for the assembly. To his surprise, he arrives at the building just as the Bible class is beginning.

Another problem facing the visitor is that of finding the appropriate classroom. He's not familiar with the building and he knows nothing of the class structure. If members don't readily suggest a certain classroom and offer to go with him to class, he may decide to forget the whole thing and go home. After all, it's easier to find the parking lot than it is to find a classroom.

Every time a visitor walks through the doors of any of our church buildings, he faces the problem of unfamiliar surroundings and procedures. Whether that visitor chooses to return or not depends on how well we respond to his uneasiness and confusion. We have to start concentrating on the incorporation process the very minute the visitor walks through the door. If he doesn't come back, you can forget about assimilating him. He'll either go somewhere else the next week or not go anywhere at all. A good rule of thumb to remember is, *never shake hands with a friend until you have greeted a stranger.*

Most of us were first-time visitors once. We had to make our way through the confusion, the misunderstanding, the miscommunication, the neglect, and the lack of sensitivity on the part of those who were already members of the congregation. Somehow we made it, but many fall by the wayside. The first time you and I walked through the doors of the church building where we now worship, we were outsiders. How were we assimilated into the fellowship of the church? What were the social and psychological dynamics that caused us to feel that we belonged in the life of the church? If we can isolate those interpersonal factors which caused us to return after the first visit and eventually led us to become involved in church activity, perhaps we can understand what has to happen if other people are to be successfully incorporated. Research into dynamics of assimilation is still in its infancy, but preliminary studies indicate that the following principles are usually observed when people start feeling that they belong.

Friendship Development

Flavil Yeakley's research on growth patterns in congregational life has documented the correlation between friendship patterns and faithfulness. He interviewed fifty Christians who were still active in the church after they had been Christians for six months. He matched the fifty faithful members against fifty persons who had been baptized but had dropped from regular attendance within six months after conversion. The results provide insight into the nature of incorporation. Every person consulted in the Yeakley survey who managed to form at least seven new friendships within the congregation remained faithful. Those who formed fewer than three friendships dropped out.[1]

Our willingness to extend friendship means the difference between spiritual life and spiritual death for many of those who have just become Christians. Yeakley concluded, "It is not enough to change what people believe and practice concerning doctrines. We must bring them into fellowship with the family of God."[2]

Sometimes Christians feel they have discharged their responsibilities to the new members when they have taught them the gospel. After all, scripture does indeed teach that the gospel is God's power for salvation (Romans 1:16). In a recent workshop on incorporation, one person asked, "If the gospel is the power of God for salvation, then what else does a Christian need? Doesn't truth account for anything?" In terms of information, the new Christian certainly needs nothing more than the Word of God. No other message has any saving power. The Scriptures warn against supplementing God's message with our own insights and theories. Severe penalties are threatened against those who would impose extra-Biblical theology on the body: "But even if we or an angel from heaven should preach to you a gospel contrary to that which we have preached to you, let him be accursed" (Galatians 1:8). Even so the written word only touches man's informational needs. Friendship meets his relationship needs.

In Paul's first letter to the church at Thessalonica, he recognizes the importance of relationship building: "But we were gentle among you, like a nurse taking care of her children. So being affectionately desirous of you, we were ready to share with you not only the gospel of God, but ourselves, because you had become very dear to us" (1 Thessalonians 2:7-8). When people hear the gospel preached, but don't see us reaching out to form caring relationships, they tend to believe that we are attempting to manipulate them. Unconditional friendship assures the new Christian that our concern is genuine.

Because there are many conflicting religious claims, many people tend to view religious teachers with a skeptical eye. Religious radio and television hucksters fill the airwaves with questionable interpretations of scripture and tasteless fundraising appeals. Pamphleteers hawk their wares through every suburban neighborhood and on every street corner. Health and wealth theology dominates the book titles in fundamentalist bookstores. Scholarly commentaries are relegated to obscure shelves at the rear of the store and always seem to sell poorly. This rather confusing and sometimes mercenary religious atmosphere complicates our objective of sharing the simple gospel with a needy world. That skepticism can be overcome through the formation of genuine, nonmanipulative friendships. As we noted earlier, "People don't care how much we know until they know how much we care."

Ministry Involvement

In Romans 16:1, Paul writes, "I commend to you our sister, Phoebe, a *servant* of the church in Cenchrea" (NIV). In verse 3 he describes Acquilla and Priscilla as "my fellow *workers* in Christ Jesus." He singles out Mary for attention in verse 6 because "she has *worked* hard among you." Urbanus is described in verse 9 as "our fellow *worker* in Christ." Tryphaena, Tryphosa, and Persis are all spoken about in Romans 16, and they are commended for their active involvement in church life.

The church exists to minister and serve. It naturally follows that those well incorporated members inevitably become involved in some avenue of ministry. They will find roles and tasks commensurate with their skills and interests. Win and Charles Arn suggest, "There is a direct relationship between the number of roles and tasks available in a church and the number of new people a church can incorporate."[3] If leadership is sensitive to new member involvement in ministry activities, then the church can be assured that it will improve its incorporation proficiency. Yeakley's research indicates that the churches which experience the greatest net growth (baptisms plus retention) are those in which the membership recognizes that there are about 55 jobs for every 100 members.[4]

As the Arns view the work of ministry, *tasks* and *roles* are two separate functions.

A "role" is an officially appointed or elected position for a person in the church, such as serving on an ad hoc committee, a board, welcoming visitors, leading a Bible study. A "task" is a special goal oriented assignment such as helping with the planning of a church worship service, helping to repave the parking lot, or working on a special missions project.[5]

One of the most difficult problems for leadership is that of knowing which roles and tasks can be assigned to new members. A person's capabilities, interests, personality, emotional maturity, and spiritual growth rate all have to be evaluated. Perhaps the greatest mistake church leaders make in mobilizing the church for action is to reserve all the meaningful roles and tasks for members who are already well established (and perhaps overinvolved) in the mainstream of church life. While this may appear to be the most prudent course because it reduces the risk of failure and embarrassment, the new Christian often feels as if he's been left with the short end of the stick. The leader who believes that he must maintain efficiency at all costs will likely be threatened by the need of new members to become involved in the ministries that count. Wisdom dictates a balance of these concerns.

Participation in Group Life

Sometimes churches decide they don't want to have small groups. Deciding to do without small groups is a little bit like deciding to do without grease while working on an automobile engine. You may have the best of intentions, but when you get through, you'd better have some hand cleaner available. Small groups are very similar. If you decide to eliminate small groups, they'll show up just as surely as grease will show up on your hands when you're adjusting the carburetor. Small groups will inevitably develop in any church of more than fifty people. Our choice is whether to wage a losing fight against them or use them to accomplish noble objectives.

Two kinds of groups are likely to be present in the membership of most churches. There will be some formal arrangement of organized groups. They may not be called small groups, but that's what they are. These include the various Bible classes, the youth group, the ladies' Bible class, the various work committees, singing groups, singles groups, and many other groups which are smaller than the entire membership but function under the control of the church's recognized leadership.

In addition to the formal group structure, practically every church has an informal group framework. Some groups develop along the lines of various social interests. Bridge players, hunters, fishermen, and other persons with similar interests often come together for recreational pursuits and end up forming friendships that blend into the rest of their lives. Some people are drawn into groups because they see other persons with similar problems who can understand how they feel about difficult circumstances in life. For example, parents of adolescent children may find themselves drawn to one another as they search for techniques of communication. Health problems, relationship problems, and personality problems draw some people together in groups. Others band together for spiritual purposes—to pray together, to study the Bible together, and to share the gospel together.

C. Peter Wagner uses the word *cell* to describe these close-knit fellowship gatherings. He believes that groups which consist of no more than eight to twelve people probably function best in developing spiritual warmth and closeness. He claims,

> It is possible to fellowship with one or two hundred other people, but it is not possible to enter into the deeper kind of interpersonal relationships that are necessary to meet another important set of human needs. The cell, sometimes called a "small group," is a very special relationship.[6]

Some Christians get a little nervous when the subject of small groups is discussed because they fear the formation of divisive cliques. Cliques are formed when people develop exclusive ideas about their group and discriminate against people who aren't in that specific group. The self-centered church members at Corinth who withheld food from hungry members when they assembled to observe the Lord's

Supper had formed a clique (See 1 Corinthians 11:17-22). Their abuse of the small group principle, however, doesn't make all groups wrong. Jesus spent most of his time with a group of twelve people.

From an incorporation point of view, a new Christian needs to be able to find a small group where he can build relationships. An incorporation-conscious church will help the new Christian find a small circle of friends in either a formal or an informal setting where a sense of belonging can be attained.

Understanding the Nature of the Church

Unfortunately we live in a confused religious climate. When most of our contemporaries think about Christianity, they visualize a denominationalized religious world. Many people have never even considered the premise that it's possible to produce an undenominational church. To their way of thinking, becoming an incorporated Christian simply means that one chooses a denominational affiliation which corresponds to personal likes and beliefs.

The New Testament describes an undenominational church. It even warns against forming sectarian bodies. When the Corinthians started choosing sides and forming parties who were loyal to certain teachers, Paul appealed for a dissolution of the sectarian spirit. He urged them to be "united in the same mind and in the same judgment" (1 Corinthians 1:10).

A well assimilated Christian will realize that he's just a Christian and that God's will directs men to respect the undenominational character of the New Testament church. Monroe Hawley has isolated five characteristics that identify a group as a denominational body:

(1) It has a legislative or executive organization foreign to God's word....(2)...it has an authoritative creed....(3)...it has a basic doctrine which contradicts the Word of God....(4)...it wears a

35

distinctive religious name which "denominates" it and separates it from others seeking to follow Christ....(5)...it possesses a sectarian attitude.[7]

By contrast, New Testament Christians are Christians only. The church is to be thought of as the body of the saved. Its boundaries are inclusive enough to take in all God's family members, but the unsaved must necessarily remain excluded. Certainly, no man has sufficient wisdom to be able to know the specific identity of all the saved, but God surely knows, and all those who are under the umbrella of his grace are members of his church, whether we who know only in part recognize them or not. Churches in the Restoration Movement were started to promote the concept of undenominational Christianity. Unfortunately, denominational thinking has become so firmly entrenched in the fabric of American religious heritage that most people never even bother to question their sectarian practices. The person who becomes fully incorporated into the church will eventually come to realize that he's just a Christian, a member of Christ's body, and he will actively resist the efforts of the world to fit him into a sectarian mold.

Assembling Regularly

Flavil Yeakley's census data reveals that there are more members of the church in many communities than the total number of those whose names are on the membership rolls of the congregations in those same localities. (See page 2.) This suggests that many people have been baptized and consider themselves members of the church, but they do not attend with any degree of regularity. They might ask a minister from the church to perform a wedding ceremony or conduct a funeral, but they really have no involvement with the local church.

A well incorporated member will not be a stranger to the other members of the church. Most congregations conduct at least three services every seven days. These include a Sunday morning service, a Sunday evening service, and a mid-week service. In practically every local congregation, the members who feel the greatest sense of belonging are those who attend all three general assemblies. From the ranks of those who attend three times every week come the elders, the deacons, the Bible school teachers, and the workers in programs and ministry. Every church has a certain number of members who attend only once each week. Some attend with even less frequency than that. Invariably church leaders will identify these infrequent attenders as the weak members. Sunday-morning-only members usually use third-person pronouns when they describe the people in the church. Such persons tend to refer to what "they" are doing, when describing programs and ministry. A person doesn't become fully assimilated until he can change "they" to "we."

Adopting a Christian Value System

The person who comes to Christ must leave behind old patterns of behavior. Paul reminds the Ephesians, "we all once lived in the passions of the flesh, following the desires of the body and mind and so were by nature the children of wrath like the rest of mankind" (Ephesians 2:3). The principle of repentance requires the child of God to adopt a new mind set and to conform to new standards of behavior. Paul pleads with his readers to "set your minds on things that are above, not on things that are on the earth" (Ephesians 3:3).

Some years ago, after many years of worldly living, a man decided to surrender his life to Jesus. His attitudes and behavior changed so radically that his friends said, "He doesn't seem like the same person." He didn't seem like the same person because he wasn't the same person. Paul suggests that a change takes place when Christ controls our lives. "Therefore if anyone is in Christ, he is a new creation, the old has passed away, behold the new has come." The man who amazed his friends by his abrupt alteration in living patterns was readily incorporated into the fellowship of the church, because he understood that his commitment involved a break with old habits, old attitudes, and even old friends. This particular man's conversion and subsequent incorporation were so complete that within a few years the church asked him to serve as a deacon, and he continues to be meaningfully involved in the life of the church.

Sometimes old habits are difficult to overcome. New insights into morality come slowly for some people. More mature Christians need to be patient with new Christians who are attempting to leave the control of Satan. Many of those who have been a part of the church throughout most of their lives have been exposed to Bible study and Christian principles since childhood. A person who becomes a Christian in mid-life doesn't have the same advantage. If Christians expect him to be on the same knowledge and behavior level as soon as he comes out of the baptistry, then Christians are expecting the impossible. We need to look behind the rough edges for attitudes of openness, searching, and submissiveness. If we really expect new Christians to grow, we must become less judgmental and more compassionate.

Evangelism Involvement

The good news about Jesus helps the lives of people only when they can hear, understand, and respond to it. The Lord has entrusted to the church the task of sharing the Word. The church is the "pillar and the bulwark of truth" (1 Timothy 3:16). The church becomes God's communication link to a lost world. The task of communicating the good news properly belongs to all members of God's family.

This is not to suggest that well incorporated Christians are all expected to master a certain commercially prepared soul-winning method. On the contrary, those church leaders who expect every Christian to become a didactic teacher of the gospel tend to display a spirit of rigidity and impracticality that's not taught in the Word of God. According to Romans 12:6, teaching is but one gift that God has bestowed on the church. In Ephesians 4:11, Paul suggests that *some* in the church are gifted as evangelists.

When we expect every Christian to become an evangelist, we are making a requirement which is both arbitrary and unscriptural. C. Peter Wagner suggests a reasonable approach to evangelistic activity when he notes, "In the average church ten percent of the members have been given the gift of evangelist."[8]

This is not to suggest that the other members are permitted to adopt a hands-off policy toward evangelism and leave the evangelistic work in the hands of those who have been gifted to teach Bible studies. First Peter 3:15 is directed to Christians in general: "Always be prepared to make a defense to anyone who calls you to account for the hope that is in you, yet do it with gentleness and reverence." There are many ways to account for one's hope in Christ. There are many techniques which can be employed in addition to the commercially prepared evangelism materials. The assimilated Christian will concern himself with sharing the hope he holds in whatever manner might be consistent with his opportunity, ability, personality, and gifts.

Conclusion

The list of incorporation characteristics can probably be expanded far beyond the ones included in this chapter. The principles mentioned are sufficient for any group of Christians to begin developing incorporation awareness. Conscientious Christians need to take inventory of the status of the incorporation dynamics that are currently present in the congregation. Are new Christians finding new friends? Are ministry roles and tasks open to them? Have they found fellowship groups where they can belong? What do their attendance records look like? How well do they comprehend the undenominational nature of the church? Have discernible changes in behavior and attitudes taken place? What is their attitude toward sharing the good news? Concrete answers to these questions provide the starting point for evaluating incorporation effectiveness.

Questions for Discussion

1. Tell what your feelings were the first time you visited the services of the church where you now worship.
2. Why did you come back?
3. What was done by the local members to help you feel that you were wanted and valued?
4. How can the people in any given church know if they are being perceived by outsiders as friendly people?
5. What principles should guide church leaders in recruiting new members for roles and tasks?
6. How can the church promote small groups in the church without encouraging cliques?
7. What methods should the church use to teach its new members the undenominational concept of the church?
8. How can we help people understand the necessity of regular worship attendance?
9. How much change should we expect in the value system of the new Christian?
10. List some ways that Christians can become evangelistically involved.

Endnotes

[1]Flavil R. Yeakley, Jr., *Why Churches Grow,* 3rd ed. (Arvada, Colorado: Christian Communications, Inc., 1979), p.54.

[2]*Ibid.,* p.110.

[3]Win and Charles Arn, *The Master's Plan for Making Disciples* (Pasadena, California: Church Growth Press, 1982), p. 150.

[4]Yeakley, *Why Churches Grow,* p. 44.

[5]Arn and Arn, *The Master's Plan for Making Disciples,* p. 157.

[6]C. Peter Wagner, *Your Church Can Grow* (Glendale, California: Regal Books, 1976), p. 107.

[7]Monroe Hawley, *Redigging the Wells* (Abilene, Texas: Quality Publications, 1976), pp. 22-23.

[8]Wagner, *Your Church Can Grow,* p. 77.

Chapter Four

What Prevents Incorporation Effectiveness?

If you're an active long-term member of the congregation where you worship, you may want to take exception to any suggestion that you may have planted hurdles to impede the progress of assimilation. Since you already feel a sense of belonging, you probably view your home congregation as an open and caring family of people who are anxious to put out the welcome mat to all newcomers. You're just so completely involved in the life of the church that you can't imagine why anyone else would feel left out. In your view, any member who says that he feels like an outsider probably chooses to be an outsider.

If you could stand in the shoes of a new member for a little while, you'd soon realize that a different point of view exists. The new member enters the church expecting to find warmth, acceptance, and fellowship, but he may soon discover that some rather formidable barriers have been strewn in his path which threaten to prevent his immediate and unqualified acceptance. Older members don't consciously plant hurdles in the path to slow down the assimilation of new members, but through their long-established friendship patterns, their expectations, their assumptions, and their language, they impede the progress of those people who make church directories obsolete by having their names added to the rolls.

In most instances these older members don't even know they are blocking the assimilation process. This chapter will challenge your ability to evaluate yourself objectively as you are asked to sensitize yourself to the perceptions of the new Christian. You'll be asked to admit your shortcomings if they do indeed exist, and you'll be urged to make necessary corrections in order to improve the incorporation effectiveness within your home congregation.

Some Christians feel that the burden of responsibility ought to be shared by both the new Christians and the older members. Of course, the new Christian must be the kind of person who truly wants a place to belong. We recognize that some seek membership in the church for devious reasons. John warns of those who "went out from us, but they were not of us, for if they had been of us they would have continued with us, but they went out that it might be plain that they all are not of us" (1 John 2:19). However, many of those who chose to leave our fellowship could have been retained if we had been more alert to their needs. We can't change the behavior of those who aren't sincere, but we can change our patterns of relating.

Relationship Patterns

In small and medium-sized churches, all the members usually know each another. In larger churches, the members tend to know a relatively small number of people—those who sit near them and those with whom they share small group identification. In the case of small and medium-sized churches, the established members have very little difficulty distinguishing members from visitors. When a new member enters their fellowship, that new member stands out like a sore thumb. At first glance, one would think that the smaller congregation would have few problems in learning to assimilate new members. Unfortunately, the social dynamics which prevail in groups affect small groups the same way they affect the larger groups, and they tend to prevent new Christians from gaining a sense of belonging. Members of small and medium-sized congregations know more about one another than names. They probably even know middle names and nicknames. They know everybody's birthdays, anniversaries, likes and dislikes. They may even know all the aunts, uncles, and cousins of longtime members. They know the make of automobile that each brother and sister in the church drives. The food, sports, and entertainment preferences of the members are common knowledge throughout the congregation. Political points of view, personal biases, and personality quirks are known to most people in the church. A well assimilated member can even diagram the seating patterns in the church auditorium and predetermine with amazing accuracy the advance seating location of each member prior to services. Pity the poor visitor who accidentally claims a longtime member's favorite pew. The longtime member usually knows which controversial subjects he can safely discuss and which ones he had better let alone unless he happens to be an iconoclast who specializes in upsetting applecarts. Through years of interaction, the older members of the congregation have come to know one another well and have learned to develop comfortable patterns of relating.

When a new member comes in, the dynamics of relating take on new and unpredictable patterns. Unless a new member belongs to an older member's extended physical family, the new Christian may find that his acceptance is rather tentative. While older members may seem friendly on the surface, they will likely avoid steering conversations into any direction in which they make themselves vulnerable.

The new member struggles with the task of getting acquainted. Putting names and faces together is hard enough, but learning which subjects are safe and which ones he shouldn't touch with a ten-foot pole doesn't come all that easily. He doesn't realize that a simple slip of the tongue labels him as a greenhorn and brings condescending stares from more knowledgeable members. His vocabulary betrays his lack of proper indoctrination when he introduces a friend to the preacher by saying, "Reverend Smith, I've been telling my friend what a wonderful pastor you are." Such a faux pas betrays one's inability to employ the terminology accepted among well established members. Some older members may even experience a slight elevation of blood pressure when they hear this "language of Ashdod." On the other hand, the older members may have learned to take the self-appointed congregational critic with a grain of salt, while the newer brothers and sisters take offense at such insensitive harshness. Older members may overlook the brother whose training in social graces has been so poorly neglected that he doesn't realize that he should eat with his fork and close his mouth while chewing. They might make allowances for the member who doesn't bathe regularly. This same kind of behavior could cause a well refined new member who has been trained to give careful attention to bodily cleansing to entertain second thoughts about continuing an association with people who tolerate poor manners and neglect personal hygiene.

Friendships

When a person enters a religious fellowship, he expects that involvement to satisfy certain needs. A new Christian who comes to Christ with sincere motives not only seeks God's forgiveness but also hopes to find acceptance in a community of loving believers. This means that a new member quite naturally hopes to find understanding, warmth, and friendship. When Christians hesitate to extend acceptance, they run the risk of pushing the new member right out the back door into spiritual delinquency.

Unfortunately, older members don't always see the need for expanding their friendships. They've already settled into comfortable friendship patterns. Taking on new friendships may threaten those relationships which already exist. The older member asks, "How can I know that my established friends will want to add another person to our friendship circle?" Forming new friendships with new Christians will most certainly require older members to alter their present schedules, and for many those new schedules are already too crowded. Sometimes older members will say, "I don't need any more friends." Besides, when someone suggests building a new friendship, it sounds like the well established member is expected to give more to the relationship than he can count on getting. Thus, while the older members may even agree that "someone" needs to reach out and form ties with the newer members, it simply doesn't occur to many of them to get personally involved in friendship development.

The Pulpit

There's also a difference in the way newer members and older members view the man in the pulpit. Most often, the newer members maintain a favorable disposition toward the preacher. The older members may accuse him of preaching canned sermons, resurrecting reruns from his files, and remaining stale in content. Even if the preacher does depend on his file, the newer members haven't heard those homilies and may think the preacher's a well informed, challenging speaker. If the preacher comes across with a reasonable degree of intelligence, remains positive, and extends warmth when he's out of the pulpit, he can count on new members to be among his most loyal supporters. Someone has observed, "Every preacher is somebody's big preacher." Many Christians look upon the first preacher they knew following their conversion as their "big preacher."

The older members have a somewhat different perspective. They compare the personality, the style, the content, and the mannerisms of the present preacher with those of former preachers who have served the congregation. Faults of the present preacher tend to become magnified, while the faults of previous preachers are dimmed in their memories with the passage of time. After a while, we think of our former preachers the same way we think about our deceased relatives. We just remember the good things. Consequently, while the newer members sing the praises of the current pulpit minister, the older members don't always share that enthusiasm.

Approaches to Ministry

The newer members tend to be more receptive to creative approaches to ministry, while the older members are often anxious to preserve traditional methods and procedures. The newer member likes to dream about great things happening in the church. Change doesn't scare him. Had he not been open to change, he would never have become a new Christian. It doesn't upset him to alter the time of the service, to conduct midweek services on Thursday night instead of Wednesday night, to dismiss the Sunday evening assembly in order to have devotional gatherings in small groups at various home locations, or to conduct the Sunday morning worship assembly without singing an invitation song. He didn't grow up with those traditions, and if they aren't visible in a certain situation, he's willing to change. Because he wants to see the church go forward, new ideas quickly win his endorsement. He's capable of originality, ingenuity, and creativity.

The older members tend to be threatened by new innovations. As a matter of fact, the term "innovation" takes on a totally negative connotation in the minds of our older members. While better informed Christians know the difference between tradition and scripture, many of them still don't like change just for the sake of change. They would say, "Don't expect us to change unless you can show us how the changes will make things better." Some fear that the slightest alterations in traditional procedures will degenerate into a rather casual attitude toward the Scriptures. In one church, a rather aggressive new member accused the leadership of getting in a rut. An elder responded, "What's wrong with being in a rut, if it's a good rut?"

Because newer members and older members tend to view change in totally different ways, the subject of change often becomes the occasion for congregational friction. When the more established members prevail in having their viewpoint adopted as a matter of congregational policy, change does not take place. Longtime members may feel they have conserved the values of the faith in their resistance to change, but the newer members may feel either that they are unwanted or that their viewpoints aren't appreciated.

Who Makes the First Move?

Because he is new, the new member tends to feel like an outsider for a long time. If the newer member is ever to gain a sense of belonging, the older members must take the first steps to assure the new brother that he is a valued, wanted, and even trusted member of the body. This kind of openness requires flexibility and even some degree of risk. Flexibility does not imply compromise of convictions. Indeed, when an older member's conviction has a solid scriptural foundation, he must not yield to the uninformed opinion of a new brother in Christ. Maturity demands defense against the attacks of Satan. "Therefore, take the whole armor of God, that you may be able to withstand in the evil day, and having done all to stand, stand therefore having girded your loins with truth, and having put on the breastplate of righteousness, and having shod your feet with the equipment of the gospel of peace; above all taking the shield of faith with which you can quench all the flaming darts of the evil one" (Ephesians 6:13-15). Some things remain in the realm of judgment, opinion, expediency, and choice of procedure. In those areas all Christians need to be open to change. Long-standing social traditions may have to give way to new patterns of behavior so that more people can feel included in the social network of the congregation. New friendships have to be formed. New ideas coming from new members must be heard and treated with respect. Sometimes we may even have to try some things that won't work. That's all right. The church is strong enough to survive our blunders. On the other hand, when wisdom and experience dictate rejection of a new member's idea, he should be told why his project can't be adopted, but never subjected to ridicule. In short, the ball is in the older member's court when it comes to helping new members develop a sense of belonging.

The Language Barrier

The language we use often hinders the incorporation of new members. While most older members would never openly oppose the practice of recruiting new members, they often find more subtle ways to express their resistance to helping develop a sense of belonging. When the average Christian is asked to express his evangelistic views, he will likely respond, "I believe we ought to teach the lost, baptize them into Christ, and then continue to teach them all things just the way it's laid out in the great commission." If you ask him about relationship building, he will probably say, "We need to reach out to new Christians with warmth and acceptance." Any Christian who doesn't agree with those statements probably believes that Ebenezer Scrooge was a prudent man and that Tiny Tim shouldn't have gotten so much sympathy.

While many Christians verbalize their willingness to open wide the doors of fellowship to all who are willing to forsake the world and walk with Jesus, their practice indicates that the opposite is sometimes true. Older Christians frequently draw lines of discrimination between themselves and those who have just entered the faith. This discrimination is more subtle than overt, but it frequently exposes itself in the vocabulary of the older members.

When the Civil Rights movement challenged the American conscience in the sixties, many Caucasians reluctantly concluded that their prejudice was reflected in their language. Black people were offended by the term "colored."

Many people who had been reared in polite white society thought they were being respectful when they talked about "colored people." In some areas of the country, the term "darky" was used as a complimentary word to describe persons of African descent, but as communication between the two races improved, white people soon learned that dark-skinned people thought they were being patronized. Many even objected to the term "Negro." Today, the word "black" is used with nearly universal acceptance on both sides of the color line. Those who used words like "colored" and "darky" really didn't think they were patronizing the black people, but then neither did they ever bother to ask black people how they felt about it. The same thing happens when a person becomes a Christian. Those who have already achieved a sense of belonging tend to use patronizing language to describe the newer members of the body. They never really stop to think how it might sound to a person who is new.

There's nothing wrong with the term "new Christian." That expression has been used several times in this book and indeed seems necessary. It serves to divide the territory between those who have not yet been fully assimilated into the fellowship and those whose acceptance is already fully assured. Even so, when we use the expression "new Christian" in a way that patronizes the person who has just found his way into the body, we tell him that he's a second-class Christian, a greenhorn who must successfully complete a period of probation before achieving real status among the members of the church.

Some time ago, a certain congregation decided to sponsor a "Campaign for Christ" in their community. Workers came from several parts of the country to canvass the locality and offer home Bible studies. As a result of that concentrated effort, several people were baptized. Almost immediately a barrier was erected between the "regular" members and the "new Christians." Public prayers emphasized the needs of the "new Christians." Announcements from the pulpit concentrated on the concern for "new Christians."

In this particular instance those who had been members prior to the campaign behaved with the very best of intentions, yet they unwittingly erected an invisible barrier by dividing the church into two classes—the new Christians and the regular members. They viewed themselves as veterans in the faith and regarded their new brothers and sisters as "rookie" members. The frequent usage of such terms as "new Christian," "campaign converts," "new converts," and similar expressions emphasized the existence of an invisible barrier to fellowship.

The pronouns "we" and "us" also convey a significant message. Church members who feel a sense of belonging invariably refer to themselves with such first-person pronouns as "we," "us," and "ours." These members expose their unannounced intention of forcing new members to pass through a probationary period by designating these new members of the fellowship with such third-person pronouns as "they," "them," and "their." While the new member of the body must expect to do some growing toward maturity in Christ, those who have already achieved higher levels of maturity must be careful to respect the new member's personhood. The Scriptures themselves refer to "new born babes" (1 Peter 2:2), and "novices" (1 Timothy 3:6 AV). We must realize that even novices are intelligent enough to know when they are being patronized, and we shouldn't be too surprised when we find them resisting efforts at manipulation.

The Homogeneous Factor

The language barrier can become a problem when the church is attempting to assimilate members from a variety of socio-economic backgrounds. The church in a certain community was made up mostly of farmers, store clerks, and blue-collar workers, but a sizable state college happened to operate in the same town. In the course of time, the elders realized that they were neglecting a great mass of teachable people on the campus, so they employed a full-time campus minister. The campus minister was successful in preaching the gospel to some of the college students, and gradually the church began to take on a different complexion. One of the disgruntled older members was heard to say, "We were doing all right until the *college element* moved in." Actually, in this particular case, the campus minister had not employed questionable evangelistic tactics. His approach was a friendship-oriented, nonmanipulative approach which the students appreciated. The problem lay in the fact that some of the older members wanted the church to remain a working-class church.

That kind of culture clash goes all the way back to the first century. In Acts 15, Luke reports on a racial and cultural conflict which developed in Jerusalem because the work Paul and Barnabas had been doing among the Gentiles had irritated some people in Jerusalem whose cultural background clashed with that of the Gentiles. "When they came to Jerusalem they were welcomed by the church and the apostles and the elders and they declared all that God had done with them. But some believers who belonged to the party of the Pharisees rose up and said, 'It is necessary to circumcise them, and to charge them to keep the law of Moses.'" (Acts 15:4-5.) The party of the Pharisees were objecting to the practices of Paul and Barnabas as they ministered among Gentiles on their first preaching tour. Throughout the chapter, the Gentiles are described by third-person pronouns. The meeting was apparently limited to Jewish believers, although Titus, a Gentile, appears to have been present (Galatians 2:1). Paul and the Jerusalem elders agreed that cultural barriers had been torn down by the intervention of God. Peter reminded them of his experience at the household of Cornelius and asserted that God "made no distinction between us and them but cleansed their hearts by faith" (Acts 15:10).

How does the church assimilate those who come into the fellowship from differing cultural settings and socioeconomic backgrounds? Leaders in the church growth movement suggest that the church should tailor its ministry to reach the homogeneous units within that fellowship. Donald McGavran relates the philosophy behind the homogeneous unit principle by observing that "people like to become Christians without crossing racial, linguistic, or class barriers."[1]

A church that follows the homogeneous unit principle in its purest form will inevitably limit its membership, because it will seek to convert only those who are socially, economically, racially, linguistically, and culturally like those who are already within the membership. The assimilation process is rather simple because new members can find others who are "their kind of people." Yeakley has observed that those whose doctrinal orientation is nearest to that found in the church of Christ are the ones who are most likely to be converted and to remain faithful.[2]

Some proponents of the homogeneous unit principle recommend that each congregation seek out a certain socio-economic class, concentrate its efforts in that direction, and let someone else worry about those in another culture. This may be possible in Southern churches, where many congregations exist within a single community representing a wide diversity of cultural, racial, and economic life styles. Even there, the principle rests on shaky ground, since it can easily become an excuse for class discrimination. The author of this work lives in a Midwestern city of more than a hundred thousand people in which there is only one church of Christ that adheres to doctrinal positions generally held by those who are in the "mainstream" of our brotherhood. We don't have the luxury of telling a black person, a welfare recipient, a person of Latin-American descent, a Pole, a Czech, a blue-collar worker, a management employee, and a professional person to go find a church that has "your kind of people." We must either assimilate these people from a wide variety of cultural backgrounds or expect them to attend denominational churches. In a few instances, we might see them go to congregations that have historical roots in the Restoration Movement, but who nonetheless would be at variance with our understanding of the truth.

The strict observance of the homogeneous unit principle has to be called into question on Biblical grounds. We have several New Testament descriptions of churches who made room for people from different levels of society. The Letter to Philemon is written for the express purpose of asking a slaveowner, Philemon, to accept his former slave, Onesimus, as a full-fledged brother in Christ. Paul pleads with his friend, "so if you consider me your partner, receive him as you would receive me" (Philemon 17). In 1 Corinthians 11, Paul rebukes the church for dividing up into homogeneous units to participate in a common meal prior to observing the Lord's Supper. Some were gorging themselves, while others went away hungry. Paul writes, "Shall I commend you in this? No, I will not" (1 Corinthians 11:22).

Shall we then throw out the homogeneous unit principle as unworkable and opposed to scripture? We have the hint of a solution in Acts 6. The Hellenists comprised a definable homogeneous unit. The apostles made no attempt to break up that unit, nor did they label it a faction. Instead, they made the entire congregation aware of the needs of that particular group and developed leadership with cross-cultural talents who could serve their needs, yet retain the good will of the entire congregation. Thus, the Hellenists kept their identity as Hellenists, but they also broadened the scope of their appreciation for other members of the Jerusalem church.

Win Arn, of the American Institute for Church Growth, opposes the homogeneous unit principle when it is used to exclude and discriminate against people.

> I disagree with those either in or out of the Church Growth Movement who suggest "churches grow best in their own homogeneous unit." I firmly believe that *"churches grow best when they heterogeneously match their community with many various homogeneous groups within the church."*[3]

While Arn concedes that a church will find it very difficult to reach a community when the membership is vastly different from the makeup of the surrounding community, he sees the church breaking itself down into smaller fellowship and ministry groups in which "various kinds of individuals can feel comfortable, accepted and loved."[4]

To make this happen, every church needs to develop persons with cross-cultural abilities, who can help people from various backgrounds find "their kind of people" within the fellowship of the local church.

When our description of those who belong to other homogeneous units begins to assume negative tones, we betray an unwillingness to work toward the assimilation of all Christians within the body. Had the apostles openly complained, "What are we going to do about this Hellenistic element?" they probably would not have pleased the whole church with their problem-solving procedure.

Conclusion

Perhaps the first step toward incorporation effectiveness lies in developing an awareness that certain barriers have been carefully constructed and often rigidly anchored in concrete. We have to be able to see these barriers before we can uproot them and tear them down. The new members usually possess 20/20 vision when it comes to seeing incorporation barriers. They can help us overcome our myopia, if we are willing to ask them.

Questions for Discussion

1. Why do older Christians tend either to deny that incorporation hurdles exist or to refuse to remove them?
2. How can we tell the difference between those who are simply discouraged because they don't seem to be able to clear the hurdles and those who "went out from us because they are not of us?"
3. How can the sensitive Christian convince other people within his own fellowship circle that the circle needs to be broadened to include some new Christians?
4. What needs of the new Christian can we legitimately and practically meet?
5. How should the older members handle the new members' enthusiasm for the preacher when the older members don't share that same enthusiasm?
6. How much credence should be given to the new members' suggestions for change?
7. How can church leaders remain open to suggestions involving change coming from new members, without driving away those members who are afraid of change?
8. What terms can we use to describe our new brethren without coming across as if we were patronizing them?
9. What is the difference between homogeneous units and cliques?
10. How can the church take advantage of the social dynamics present in homogeneous units without practicing discrimination?

Endnotes

[1]Donald McGavran, *Understanding Church Growth* (Grand Rapids, Michigan: William B. Eerdmans Publishing Company, 1970) p. 98.

[2]Flavil R. Yeakley, Jr., *Why Churches Grow*, 3rd ed. (Broken Arrow, Oklahoma: Christian Communications, Inc., 1979), p. 22.

[3]Win Arn, "A Fresh View of the Homogeneous Unit Concept," in *The Win Arn Church Growth Report* (Pasadena, California: The American Institute for Church Growth, 1983), Vol. I, No. 1, pp. 2-3.

[4]*Ibid.*

Chapter Five

The Tie That Binds Us Together

Although we can nearly always improve our incorporation effectiveness, the fact remains that no church is really capable of incorporating every person in any given community who sincerely wants to find a church home. Certain dynamics flow through the fabric of church life which attract some people and repel others. Schaller explains,

> Every long established congregation is organized around one or more principles which weld a loose collection of individuals into a cohesive group. Once a congregation passes the 35 to 50 mark in worship attendance, this glue becomes an important factor in understanding the distinctive characteristics of each congregation. As time passes, one form of glue is replaced by a new organizing principle which rallies people together and unites—or reunites—them as one fellowship. Whenever one of these components referred to as glue, disappears, either it is replaced or that congregation begins to diminish in vitality, enthusiasm, size and outreach.[1]

Churches of Christ pretty well follow the pattern of other religious fellowships in this respect. The organizing principles that either cause a person to feel a sense of belonging or a sense of rejection may differ from those felt in other religious bodies, but the fact remains that the *dynamics* of inclusion and exclusion are at work in every congregation. A person who wants to be effective in helping new members develop a sense of belonging will want to know what those principles are. This chapter will identify some of those characteristics.

Organizing Principles

1. *Loyalty to Restoration Ideals.* In 1980, Dr. Mac Lynn of the Harding Graduate School of Religion in Memphis, Tennessee, completed an extensive study of the numerical strength within Churches of Christ.[2] He was able to identify 12,945 congregations, with a total membership of 1,245,540, in the United States.[3] While there are many differences of conviction among the members of these churches, we generally hold the following convictions in common: We baptize for the remission of sins, observe the Lord's Supper every Sunday, organize ourselves as independent congregations without a central governing board, and omit the use of instrumental music in our worship services. From a sociological viewpoint, we are descendants of the work done by Thomas and Alexander Campbell, Barton W. Stone, and others during the early part of the nineteenth century. The Stone-Campbell movement centered around the twin emphases of religious unity and the restoration of New Testament Christianity. In what amounts to a practical denial of the first objective, the movement has splintered into three main groups, the Disciples of Christ, the Independent Christian Churches, and the noninstrumental Churches of Christ.

Churches of Christ continue to function as self-governing, independent churches without any organizational ties. Even so, such a spirit of commonality exists among them that when one member moves from one part of the country to another, he has no difficulty recognizing a church that is like the one he just left. That's because these churches adhere to certain doctrinal tenets which are referred to as "the Restoration Principle." Bill J. Humble provides this succinct sketch of restoration concepts:

> (1) The Bible is the inspired Word of God and the final authority for God's people. (2) The New Testament is a divine pattern or constitution for the church of Christ. (3) Whenever this pattern is followed, the church will be restored just as it was in the New Testament era. (4) A chain of true churches stretching back through the centuries is not essential to our being the true church. The only essential is the New Testament, for whenever it is followed, the church will be like the New Testament pattern. (5) The churches which follow the New Testament pattern will have the same worship, organization, etc. and will therefore be one.[4]

A person who is committed to those ideals may be willing to tolerate circumstances that are otherwise undesirable, simply because those ideals are of paramount importance to him. He doesn't want to worship with a church that holds dissimilar views about the nature of Christianity. This also explains why people sometimes drive thirty or forty miles to worship and pass a dozen church buildings before they arrive at their destination. Their loyalty to the restoration principle supersedes such concerns as distance and convenience.

This doctrinal loyalty is so deeply ingrained into the lives of the members that a unique vocabulary has developed among people with restoration loyalties. New members don't "join the church," they "obey the gospel." The man in the pulpit may be called a "preacher," a "minister," or an "evangelist," but unless he is also an elder, he will not be called a "pastor." As a practical matter of fact, restoration churches rarely use the term "pastor" at all, even though it has Biblical sanction.

Other terms have developed through social custom. Churches of Christ usually don't conduct "revivals." We hold "gospel meetings." Some older members refer to them as "protracted meetings." Church members don't attend "conventions" and "conferences," but we do go to "lectureships" and "workshops." Elders oversee congregations, but no one ever calls them "the board." Worship takes place in "the auditorium" and not in the "sanctuary." A well indoctrinated member can usually tell whether he's among brethren very quickly simply by listening to religious terminology. I once met a salesman who called on ministers of varying religious persuasions. When he learned of my church affiliation, he said, "Please don't brief me on terminology." Apparently someone already had! While some of the lingo we have developed may be rather arbitrary and even reactionary, it serves the useful function of helping members to be able to recognize a fellowship of people where they can expect to achieve a sense of belonging.

2. *Regional and National Roots.* Although I am a native Texan, my home is in Iowa. I never worry about the acceptance of my Texas drawl because at least half the congregation has Southern roots. Churches of Christ have concentrated their numerical strength in the South and the Southwest. Consequently, when members move about in our highly mobile society, they not only look for a church home where adherence to restoration principles can be found, but they also look for cultural acceptance.

A young man from Texas found himself living temporarily in the Pacific Northwest. On Sunday, he found a building with a sign out front which read, "Church of Christ." However, when he went inside, he observed a service that appeared strange to him. He was particularly upset by the presence of an organ. Later that day, he got on the telephone and called churches that were listed in the yellow pages under "Churches of Christ." At one church, a man answered the phone with a deep Texas drawl. The young man felt better, but he was still skeptical. He said, "Now I want to know, is this the real church of Christ?" The man on the other end of the line laughed and said, "Son, it's just like what you've got back in Texas."

Quite often a person's place of origin becomes a factor in his acceptance. Several years ago, a young engineer just out of college was sent from his home in Texas to train for his employment in a certain Midwestern city. In the course of time, he happened to meet the preacher for the church there. The preacher was also a Texas native, and before long these two "good ole boys" were reminiscing about things back home. The young engineer became curious about the church. A study ensued and he was baptized into Christ. He now lives in his home state and serves as the youth minister for the congregation where he worships.

A person from the South who comes into the congregation where I worship will find a little island of acceptance. He may get invited home for black-eyed peas and okra, or he may go to the home of a native Texan who serves the best plate of Mexican food this side of Dallas. As a result, our ability to incorporate Southerners who have migrated to our community is quite commendable. On the other hand, we are faced with the knowledge that seventy percent of the people who live in our state are native-born Iowans. It's also quite likely that upwards of ninety percent of them have lived all their lives in the Upper Midwest. To these Midwesterners, "beans" doesn't refer to "pinto beans," it means "soybeans." Football fans don't understand expressions like "Roll Tide" and "Hook 'em Horns," but they proudly display bumper stickers that read "How 'Bout Them Hawks." An automobile driver who displays a rebel flag and honks a horn that plays "Dixie" is out of place, but if the horn plays the University of Iowa fight song, that's a different matter entirely.

Most of the people in my home congregation have Anglo-Saxon surnames, but many residents of our community have German surnames. Members of the Lutheran church, just down the street, can remember when most of the services were conducted in the German language. German traditions remain very much alive in our community. Besides that, strong religious family ties tend to preserve loyalties to Lutheran and Catholic traditions. A predominantly Anglo-Saxon church with a strong Southern flavor in its membership has its work cut out for it in attempting to attract and assimilate new members from the community.

3. *The Personality of the Preacher.* While some Christians will stay with a congregation through innumerable pulpit changes, there is always some shifting around when the church changes preachers. Some members prefer a didactic style of preaching which focuses on issues and arguments. Members who are attracted to this pulpit style often expect the man in the pulpit to confirm their biases while attacking the views of those who disagree with them. They want the preacher to slay some kind of theological dragon every time he enters the pulpit, but they prefer not to be caught in the dragon's shoes themselves. There is another type of didactic preacher who specializes in expository preaching. The preaching of such well-known denominational pulpiteers as John MacArthur, Jr., and Charles Swindoll has popularized the expository approach in our own brotherhood. Expository preaching can also vary in style. Swindoll prefers finding practical applications from the text (sometimes at the risk of context), while MacArthur bombards his audiences with meticulous explanations of Greek word meanings, tenses, and idioms. Both men are quite successful, speaking each Sunday to hundreds of listeners, but their audiences have different preferences.

Some preachers concentrate on the problems of daily living. In the denominational world, Robert Schuller and Ray Stedman are two very popular preachers with radically different methods of concentrating on practical problems. Schuller uses very little scripture and emphasizes a message that consists mostly of how to succeed in the material world, while Stedman is much more scripture-oriented, but still manages to identify with the struggles of the common man.

Congregations can and do flourish numerically under all these styles of preaching, but a certain style invariably attracts a certain kind of member. The worst thing the leadership can do from an incorporation viewpoint is to drastically change the pulpit style. If a church has been listening to a preacher who concentrates on finding Bible answers to the problems of modern society, and then suddenly switches to a fire-breathing iconoclast who never enters the pulpit without attacking something, that church will likely experience an assimilation problem followed by a dropout problem.

The same thing can also be said when the situation is reversed. However, the problem isn't really severe in that case because life related preaching sprinkled with vivid illustrations attracts more people than dogmatic, argumentative preaching. The "attack" approach makes many people uncomfortable. I recently ran a survey in the congregation where I preach, and only one person expressed the desire for me to adopt a more didactic and more belligerent stance.

The late Ira North described the demise of a congregation where a radical change in pulpit styles took place:

> His attitude is hostile and negative and the pulpit resounds with scathing denunciations of everybody and everything. Those attending are browbeaten for those who do not attend. They leave despondent and discouraged and the inevitable begins to happen. The members are slipping away.[5]

Yeakley contends that the preacher fulfills a crucial function in the church growth process. He suggests, "The preacher is the most important factor in projecting the image of the congregation."[6] Those churches where the growth rate is high are those that tend to employ preachers whose pulpit style is positive, while those who employ preachers with a negative style tend to experience a low net growth rate.

From an incorporation point of view, Yeakley's research

implies that more new members are likely to develop a sense of belonging if they hear a positive message from the pulpit.

The preacher's personality outside the pulpit is also important. In some cases, a pleasant demeanor outside the pulpit can make up for lack of competence on the platform. A preacher who acts responsibly in the community, gives of himself unselfishly toward serving the needs of people, and helps the members with problem solving may indeed be the reason why many people stay with a congregation.

4. *Family Ties.* Fleshly kinship must be considered one of the organizing principles of fellowship in the church. We like to think of ourselves as the family of God. We use such terms as "brother" and "sister" as a replacement for "Mr." and "Mrs." Some consider it a theological error to capitalize the word "brother," even when it is used as a form of address. However much we may attempt to endorse the idea of belonging to a spiritual family, the fact remains that it doesn't always work out that way in actual practice. Sometimes, as the saying goes, "blood is thicker than water."

Some congregations are built almost entirely around two or three family clans. When a church is dominated by two or three families, those families generally have control of the leadership. About the only way a person can develop a sense of belonging in that kind of church is either to be born into one of the predominant families or to marry into one of them.

In congregations where the membership is about evenly divided between those who belong to family clans and those who have no kinship ties within the congregation, an unhealthy tension sometimes arises. The kinfolk factor is perhaps the most difficult of all incorporation problems to solve.

5. *The Nature of the Worship.* Churches of Christ differ from most other religious fellowships in that we omit the use of instrumental music from our assemblies. We do so on the grounds of conscience, contending that the use of instrumental music lacks Biblical authority.

Most new members struggle through an uncomfortable adjustment period before they get used to a cappella singing. The same problem exists for those who have grown up in a worship environment characterized by a highly structured, formal liturgy. Our services vary considerably from the program of worship that features a prepared litany. Some people think we approach God much too casually and irreverently. It makes some new Christians so uncomfortable they make statements like "I don't feel like I've been to church." While the way one feels about the style of the service doesn't determine its acceptance in God's eyes, if we want to avoid losing new Christians in the first year after their conversion, we must learn how to be sensitive to their prior conditioning. If a person is accustomed to hearing the sounds of an organ in worship, he simply can't be expected to feel comfortable with our style of singing until he's had time to adjust. Those who have successfully made the transition can be helpful in explaining why things are done in a certain way. All of us must learn to demonstrate patience and understanding.

The problem of worship style also affects church members as they move from one congregation to another in today's mobile society. Many of our congregations retain a rural flavor. This is even true in some large cities, where rural folk have migrated to urban centers in search of employment. Many of these people prefer that hymns be rendered in a simple musical style, and they prefer to dress casually. Some can recall when the "singing convention" was one of the more popular forms of entertainment. They prefer a hymnbook which contains songs written in that manner and feel more at home with Albert E. Brumley than they do with Beethoven or even Isaac Watts.

Others have more refined musical tastes. We have hymnbooks available which include the scores of Handel, Bach, and Beethoven, along with the works of Fanny J. Crosby and P. P. Bliss. Such hymnals generally avoid the tunes written by V. O. Stamps and Mosie Lister. When a church member who has been singing Southern gospel tunes all his life moves to a church that sings Bach, dissatisfaction sometimes surfaces. A few congregations have recognized that a variety of cultural tastes exist, and the leadership instructs songleaders to accommodate the various cultural interests of the church.

6. *Other factors.* Many other factors enter into a congregation's ability to help new members achieve a sense of belonging. Some aren't as important as others, but the accumulation of a number of these factors may tip the balances of the scales for or against assimilation.

Social class becomes a unifying factor in most congregations. Churches of Christ generally haven't done very well in assimilating either the very poor or the very rich. In some congregations, social class may be the predominant organizing principle. This seems to be true more in denominational churches than within the Churches of Christ. In some cities, the professional people and the local politicians will tend to migrate toward one church, while the blue-collar people end up somewhere else, with welfare recipients being left over for those churches which specialize in rescue mission types of ministries.

A *crisis* in the lives of the members can be a unifying factor. The tragic death of a teenage girl in one congregation led to numerous conversions and restorations. Sickness and natural disasters sometimes draw people together.

Achievable goals help create oneness in a congregation fragmented by diversity of talent, temperament, and personality. They can also ignite a burning fire in a congregation that has grown cold with lethargy. Goals will be a negative factor, however, if the majority of the congregation disagrees with the goals which the established leadership has outlined. The goals have to be owned by a large cross section of the membership.

Community involvement can be a rallying point. Sometimes churches build their identification around a crusade to eliminate some kind of social or moral evil such as immoral television programming or pornographic literature. The avowed intention to make a difference in public policy becomes an organizing principle.

Building location will be a factor for some. Most church

growth experts say that the church's primary ministry area lies within a twenty-minute drive from the church building. People who live outside that perimeter may be active in the church themselves, but they will find it difficult to influence their neighbors to become a part of a church that is more than a twenty-minute drive from their homes. Thus a congregation should concentrate its efforts in the immediate vicinity.

The Inevitability of Exclusion

Although we might choose to believe that our doors are open to all people, most congregations have unintentionally chosen to exclude certain persons from the membership. If the services of a congregation are conducted only in English, then it is only logical to assume that for all practical purposes the doors of that church remain closed to those who don't use English as their primary language. Our country has become such an international community that people with foreign ethnic origins make up the majority of the population in certain larger cities. Churches must assess this rapidly changing social dynamic in the light of the mandate of the Great Commission which urges us to "go therefore and make disciples of all nations" (Matthew 28:19).

Are there deaf persons residing in your community? If there's no one in the congregation to sign for the deaf, you can't realistically expect to assimilate them into the life of the church. Those who have studied the deaf ministry have learned that there's more to successful assimilation than being able to communicate in sign language. Someone has to take the initiative to understand the social principles present in deaf families.

If a church auditorium can be reached only by climbing some twenty or thirty steps up a steep incline, then that particular congregation has probably closed its doors to those who get around in wheelchairs. As a matter of fact, such a church has probably closed its doors to many of the elderly who simply can't manage twenty or thirty steps.

Those church buildings with high steps in front of the entrance were built at a time when most of the people who attended church lived in the neighborhood, walked to the church services, and had plenty of stamina to climb the steps. We live in a different kind of environment.

When the church decides to respond to the needs of any special group of people, it automatically excludes another group that has different needs. The church doesn't usually do this through sinister and unhealthy motives. The problem stems from the differences in people. Church leaders must decide which groups they can serve best. As they do so, they must realize that their decision will inevitably exclude some people. No one congregation has the capability of programming for the need of every person in any sizable community.

Conclusion

If we want new members of the congregation to feel a sense of belonging, we will have to come to some kind of understanding about the kind of needs we can expect to meet with the talent we presently have. We will need to target that group and concentrate our efforts among them. There will always be a few persons who are broad enough in their thought patterns to be able to relate to people of more than one culture. Praise God for cross-cultural members. They will become the key people who will help us enlarge our vision and target new groups with our evangelistic outreach. We limit ourselves severely if we decide we want to reach only one particular socioeconomic group, or one need-oriented group, or one racial group, but we shouldn't waste time punishing ourselves with guilt because we lack the ability to help each and every subgrouping of the population that might exist in a given community.

Questions for Discussion

1. What does Lyle Schaller mean when he uses the term "glue"?
2. How does the restoration principle provide a strong bonding element within the Churches of Christ?
3. How large a role does restoration "social culture" play in our loyalty to the local church?
4. How do the regional and national-origin factors function in the church where you worship?
5. What can be done to ensure the incorporation of members who do not belong to a prominent family clan?
6. How can we help people who come into our fellowship from liturgical churches to adjust to our worship structure?
7. Why does the personality of the preacher influence the incorporation of new members?
8. How can we accommodate various worship styles while remaining true to the Scriptures in the way we conduct worship?
9. To what extent does social class determine the makeup of the church where you worship?
10. Why is it inevitable that every congregation will exclude some sincere seekers of truth from its membership?

Endnotes

[1]Lyle E. Schaller, *Assimilating New Members* (Nashville, Tennessee: Abingdon Press, 1979), pp. 22-23.

[2]Mac Lynn, ed., *Where the Saints Meet* (Austin, Texas: Firm Foundation Publishing House, 1982), p. v.

[3]*Ibid.*, p. ix.

[4]Bill J. Humble, *The Story of the Restoration* (Austin, Texas: Firm Foundation Publishing House, 1969), p. 24.

[5]Ira North, *Balance, A Tried and Tested Formula for Church Growth* (Nashville, Tennessee: Gospel Advocate, 1983), p. 15.

[6]Flavil R. Yeakley, Jr., *Why Churches Grow,* 3rd ed. (Broken Arrow, Oklahoma: Christian Communications, Inc., 1979), p. 49.

Chapter Six

The Importance of Fellowship

Let's look at the fellowship patterns in a typical church. Our typical congregation, which we shall name Westside, started in 1955 as a result of a church planting project orchestrated by the Downtown congregation. The Westside membership directory lists two hundred seventy names. The leadership has been reticent to remove names from the roll, so the membership list contains the names of some thirty members who haven't attended services for at least a year. Twenty-five others normally attend about once a month. About seventy-five members can be counted on to attend on Sunday mornings, but they do not attend the other services and they usually don't involve themselves in the social life of the church and its ministry opportunities. Most of the others attend Sunday mornings, Sunday evenings, and Wednesday evenings with varying degrees of regularity. Involvement ranges from such minimal contributions as serving the Lord's Supper to active participation in personal evangelism.

About twenty per cent of those who attend regularly have no kind of ministry involvement. Fifty percent are involved minimally, and about twenty percent are heavily involved. If you ask those whose attendance and involvement patterns are somewhat erratic and feeble to describe the fellowship of the church, their reaction will most likely be negative. These minimally involved members may concede that the preaching from the pulpit is sound and that the worship is conducted according to Biblical principles, but they do not view the church as a warm, close-knit, caring support system. They tend to feel excluded from the inner workings of the church. They don't participate in decision making at any level, and they have a very low sense of belonging.

Ask the same question of those who are heavily involved and you will probably receive positive statements about the fellowship of the church. The difference between the two groups exists because the former group has achieved church membership without deepening fellowship ties, while the latter group has broken through the barriers that would prevent fellowship.

Fellowship and Membership

In our brotherhood, we tend to use those two terms synonymously. A person's name appears on the membership roll because he is in "full fellowship" with the body of Christ. To say that we are in fellowship with another person is tantamount to agreeing to regard that person as a Christian. Rarely is the term "fellowship" used to describe the intellectual, emotional, and spiritual sense of belonging a person feels when he becomes fully incorporated into the body of Christ.

The New Testament, however, does use the term in the latter sense. The term *koinonia* "denotes the share one has in anything, a participation, a fellowship recognized and enjoyed. Thus it is used to describe the common experiences and interests of Christian men."[1] The early Christians developed a unique bond of oneness which needs to be felt in the church today. The Jerusalem church developed such a strong sense of interdependence that "all who believed were together and had all things common" (Acts 2:42). When Christians moved from place to place, their sense of commonality was so strong that they anxiously sought the strengthening of fellowship ties. After Saul of Tarsus was converted, he sought the fellowship of the disciples in Jerusalem. Because of his reputation, many of the disciples were reluctant to welcome him, "but Barnabas took and brought him to the apostles and declared to them how on the road he had seen the Lord, who spoke to him and how at Damascus he had preached boldly in the name of Jesus. So he went in and out among them at Jerusalem" (Acts 9:27-39). Saul became a member of the body of Christ when he was baptized at Damascus, but he was not received into practical fellowship among his brethren in Jerusalem until Barnabas appointed himself to the role of fellowship facilitator.

Fellowship also extends to the acts that are carried out as a consequence of the existence of a relationship bond between Christians. Paul seemed to enjoy a special emotional attachment to the Philippian church. He declared his affection for the church in the early part of the epistle: "I thank my God in all my remembrance of you, always in every prayer of mine, making my prayer with joy, thankful for your partnership in the gospel from the first day until now" (Philippians 1:3-5). In chapter 4, he indicates that this partnership went beyond feeling to an expression of tangible action in the form of financial support: "And you Philippians yourselves know that in the beginning of the gospel when I left Macedonia, no church entered into partnership with me in giving and receiving, except you only" (Philippians 4:16).

The church growth literature employs the term "fellowship" to describe a sense of belonging and acceptance which a person feels after he has truly become bonded to the other members of the congregation. Lyle Schaller believes that every congregation operates with two different sets of dynamics. One set of dynamics he calls "the membership circle." Every legitimate member of the church belongs inside that circle. The second set of dynamics concerns a "fellowship circle." "The fellowship circle includes the members who feel a sense of belonging and who feel fully accepted into the fellowship of that called out community."[2]

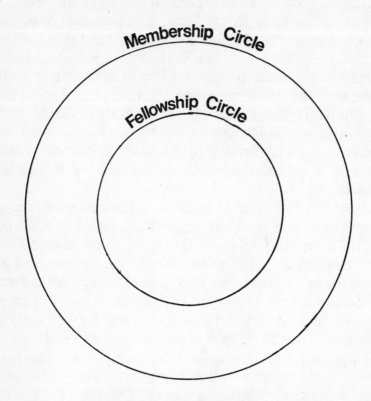

Schaller's Membership Circle

C. Peter Wagner uses the term "congregation" to describe more or less the same thing. "The major characteristic of a congregation as I see it, is that everyone is supposed to know everyone else. Here is where fellowship starts, although it does not end here."[3] In chapter 3 we noted a correlation between friendship patterns and continued involvement with the church. If a person doesn't make any new friends within the first year of his conversion, he is not likely to remain active in the church. That being the case, it also follows that a new Christian must find his way into the fellowship circle of the church within the first year of his conversion. If he does not do so, he is likely to become inactive.

Why Some People Feel Left Out of the Fellowship Circle

1. *Negative conversion techniques.* Flavil Yeakley suggests that some of our approaches to evangelism actually work against relationship building. He characterizes one of the more popular approaches as a "manipulative monologue."[4] Essentially, the manipulative monologue may be thought of as a sales approach. Most of the commercial personal evangelism materials being marketed today lend themselves to use as tools for someone who desires to employ a manipulative monologue. Certainly these materials can be used in a different way, but often they are not. Some approaches may be classified as a manipulative dialogue since two people are talking to each other, but the answers to be given by the "prospect" are really programmed in advance. Certain clever psychological ploys are used to elicit certain desired responses. When these techniques are used, people are often baptized at the close of the so-called "studies," but soon have second thoughts about what they have done. When a person has been sold the gospel with the same methods that sales persons use to sell automobiles or refrigerators, that recently baptized person sometimes feels he's been sold a product he really didn't want to buy. He just didn't know how to say, "No." He develops a case of the buyer's blues and starts looking for a way to back out on his commitment. When we have something as precious as the gospel to present, we should not be so manipulative in our zeal to persuade people as to make them feel they have been "ripped off." Paul reminds us, "For we are not, like so many, peddlers of God's word, but as men of sincerity, as commissioned by God, in the sight of God we speak in Christ" (2 Corinthians 2:17). Yeakley discovered that sixty-nine percent of those who were baptized after a presentation which they perceived to be manipulative dropped out of the church within a year.[5]

Some of those who presented the gospel were seen as

transmitters of information. The person receiving the gospel message tended to view the person telling the message primarily as a teacher. The teachers were far more successful in retaining their newly won students, but most of their pupils said, "No, thank you," when they were asked about being baptized. Seventy-five percent of those who responded in Yeakley's research project indicated that they declined the invitation to become Christian when they saw the person presenting the gospel as a teacher.[6]

On the other hand, when the person presenting the gospel used a nonmanipulative dialogue as his method of presenting the gospel, only four percent of those who were converted dropped out of the church. These people saw the one presenting the message as a friend, genuinely interested in building a relationship of trust and mutual respect. People are intelligent enough to see through traps, ploys, and gimmicks which are designed to lure them into becoming Christians, and they tend to resent being used. On the other hand, there is enough awareness of personal emptiness and feeling of spiritual need that the world is literally filled with people who will be very accepting of the gospel message once they understand that the person presenting it truly wants to be a friend and truly wants to assist them with the task of living.

Part of the problem may be attributed to the fact that evangelistic presentations often take place with people who have never had exposure to Christians prior to their conversion. Sometimes a person enters the building for the very first time when he comes to be baptized. His only contact with the church has been through the person who has been presenting the gospel message, and that has been quite limited because the conversation has been confined to the subject matter presented in the study. It's going to be extremely difficult to assimilate a person like that, especially if most of the conversation has consisted of a monologue on the part of the evangelist. Win and Charles Arn contribute this thoughtful insight into the assimilation process:

The incorporation process of a new disciple actually starts long before the person joins the church. The friendships established with others in the church earlier, now serve as a natural bridge into the worshiping congregation.[7]

When a Christian goes out to study with a non-Christian, he must realize that conversation about family, occupation, hobbies, recreation, and social interests constitutes a vital part of the relationship building process. One must not think that he's wasting time if he doesn't get right into the lesson during the first fifteen minutes of a visit. Friendship develops through shared experiences—meals taken together, recreational activities enjoyed together, sorrows shared, small talk, and personal concern about what goes on in the life of somebody else.

John R. W. Stott surely pricks the conscience of many a would-be soul winner when he comments:

He sends us *into the world.* For he was sent into the world. He did not touch down like a visitor from outer space, or arrive like an alien bringing his own alien culture with him. No, he took to Himself our own humanity, our flesh and blood. He actually became one of us and experienced our frailty, our suffering, our temptation, our death.

And now he sends us "into the world" to identify with others as he identified with us, to become as vulnerable as He did. It is surely one of our more characteristic evangelical failures that we have seldom taken seriously this principle of incarnation. . . . It comes more natural to us to shout the gospel at people from a distance than to involve ourselves deeply in their lives, to think ourselves into their problems and to feel with them in their pains.[8]

The social gatherings of the church also provide an opportunity for the development of significant relationships. When nonmembers attend a barbeque, a wedding celebration, a costume party, a picnic, or some other purely social function, they have the privilege of getting to know Christians in an area where they can feel they are on more or less common ground. A Bible class may be more threatening because the nonmember doesn't even know how to find First Corinthians, much less discuss the finer points of exegesis to be covered in the class. Some of that threat can be removed when he learns that Christian people have hurts, feelings, weaknesses, and ordinary human problems. Nearly every church finds some occasion for its members to get together socially. These social functions provide an opportunity for the nonmember to see the humanness of the Christian family, and that will pay dividends down the road when the church is attempting to assimilate those new members into the body. As Yeakley has reminded us,

> When a person has no meaningful contact with the congregation in the process of his conversion, he is likely to feel no meaningful sense of identification with the congregation after his conversion, therefore he is likely to drop out.⁹

2. *The heterogeneous factor.* People tend to feel left out of the fellowship circle when they perceive the makeup of the membership to be too different from them. A few years ago, the Hilltop church (so named for the sake of this discussion) conducted a door-to-door campaign utilizing workers from other areas of the country. The members at Hilltop had anticipated a large influx of new members. Several people were baptized during the campaign effort, and a marvelous spirit of oneness prevailed between the host congregation and the temporary workers.

The brethren at Hilltop knew they had to be prepared to assimilate new members. They diligently prepared themselves to teach the "new converts material" which had been left behind by the campaign workers. As they had anticipated, a large number of people were baptized during the concentrated effort. When the workers left, the local members at Hilltop set about diligently in a concentrated effort to help these new Christians grow. They prayed fervently for their spiritual development. Follow-up studies took place in several homes throughout the area. Those who had committed themselves to helping new Christians grow invited these new brothers and sisters into their homes. An effort was put forth to see that all the new members received special invitations to the various social functions. Various forms of assistance were provided by the older members in helping some of the newer brethren deal with life's problems.

However, it soon became apparent that most of the new members were feeling left out. Gradually their attendance patterns began to slip, and within three years nearly all of those who had been won during the campaign had either returned to their previous spiritual commitments or reverted to a life of nonreligious activity.

The elders at Hilltop agonized over the situation. They had made a concentrated effort to evangelize their community and to assimilate those new members who had become Christians. The leaders felt the congregation had done a good job in getting ready for the campaign and in preparing themselves to minister to the needs of new Christians. Unfortunately, the new members didn't stay. Their gradual exodus took its toll on the morale of the church, a period of decline set in, and evangelistic zeal waned.

As the leadership evaluated their disappointment, they soon realized that assimilation failure was built into the evangelistic method they had chosen. With the very best of intentions, they had fallen into the trap suggested by Yeakley when he discovered that persons without meaningful contact with the church prior to conversion are likely to drop out later on. The limited amount of relationship building that occurs in a campaign setting prior to baptism usually involves a worker who lives at some far distant place. It is very difficult to transfer a friendship built in that kind of atmosphere from the campaign worker to a resident member.

The elders also came to recognize that they were leading a middle-class congregation consisting mostly of Caucasians from wage-earning families. Most of those who were baptized during the campaign represented a different cultural and socioeconomic background. Many of those baptized during the campaign received some kind of public financial assistance for their economic support. Few of them owned automobiles, which meant that the Hilltop members would be called on to transport them to the services. The Hilltop brethren also learned that they would often be called upon to provide transportation in other circumstances, some of which were questionable. After a while members of the congregation began to suspect they were being used by some of the new members. To their credit, however, the Hilltop members made a devoted and valiant effort to cross these cultural lines through service, fellowship, and understanding. They invited new members into their homes and saw to it that they had transportation for church services, the social gatherings of the services, and even other occasions. Unfortunately, when the new members began to realize that most of the people who attended Hilltop had good paying jobs, lived in nice three-bedroom suburban houses, drove late-model cars, and could afford to bring such expensive dishes as rolled rump roast to a potluck gathering, the new members felt intimidated, inferior, and out of place.

Most of the Hilltop members live in traditional American families. The father is present in the home and serves as the principal breadwinner. The wife and mother may have a part-time job, but if there are small children still at home, she probably spends most of her time taking care of the family's domestic needs. Little do the Hilltop members realize that the norm in their fellowship is not the norm in American society. According to John Naisbitt, "today only a distinct minority (7 percent) of America's population fits the traditional family profile."[10] The members at Hilltop naively believed they would baptize mostly married couples during their campaign effort. As it turned out, not a single new member fit the traditional family profile. The Hilltop members found themselves dealing with families where numerous children were present in a family that had no resident father. In some instances children didn't even know their father's identity. Stepchildren, half-brothers, and half-sisters complicated some family arrangements. With all these sociological differences, the Hilltop congregation soon discovered that the road to assimilation was too high a hill to climb.

Today, the Hilltop church remembers its campaign experience with mixed feelings. They recall with great fondness the enthusiasm engendered by the concentrated effort. They learned much from the dedication of the visiting workers, but there's also a feeling of sadness because the campaign didn't produce long-term church growth. Today the church is moving in the direction of implementing "friendship evangelism." While no spectacular successes have been recorded, the church usually manages to hold those who are converted. Sometimes the people who are converted have some special problem, but the social and cultural distance between the newer members and the older members is considerably less than it was with those people who had been won through the campaign effort. The Hilltop leaders have accepted one of Donald McGavran's premises:

> The faith spreads most naturally and contagiously along the lines of the social network of living Christians, especially new Christians. Receptive, undiscipled men and women usually receive the possibility when the invitation is extended to them from credible friends, relatives, neighbors, and fellow workers from within their social web.[11]

The Hilltop leaders, however, should not content themselves with maintaining a homogeneous church. The ministry area around the Hilltop building contains people with much greater diversity than the church itself. The church needs to reflect the sociological makeup of its community. If the Hilltop leaders will look carefully at the congregation they guide, they will discover a sprinkling of dependable families whose social and cultural makeup resembles that of some of the people they lost after the campaign. Somehow these people made their way into the fellowship circle at Hilltop despite the fact that their life styles are at variance with those of most of the members. Unfortunately, these cross-cultural people have never been given significant tasks and roles. If Hilltop truly wants to minister to the needs of the people in the vicinity of the church building, the leadership must realize that these cross-cultural people hold the key that will unlock the doors of evangelistic success in other sociological settings. These people must be trained and developed to spearhead ministry efforts in areas where the Hilltop outreach has been only minimally successful. Such people must become the core of new classes and groups.

3. *Church conflict*. Despite the Lord's prayer for unity in John 17, some churches are badly splintered. Personality feuds, one-upmanship games, and bitter infighting have no place in the Lord's church, but one would have to be extremely naive to believe that such ungodly behavior is completely absent from the church.

When a new member comes into the body, he doesn't know that a long-standing internal church rivalry has divided the church family into warring camps. He innocently wanders through the fellowship oblivious to the fact that his association with one group of people will cause him to be ostracized by another group. After all, the combatants in this form of warfare don't wear uniforms, so it's hard to tell who belongs on which side when a person is the newest member of a church group.

Within a very short time, however, the new member is likely to discover that certain antagonists have been at one another's throats for years and the issues really don't seem all that earthshaking:

Brother X didn't attend Sister Y's daughter's wedding and Sister Y doesn't speak to Brother X.

Sister A wasn't asked to host the preacher for lunch during the last gospel meeting. She has her feelings hurt and won't attend services.

Nobody came to see Brother B when he was in the hospital last spring, so he tells everyone how badly the church mistreated him. Of course, Brother B didn't tell anyone he was in the hospital.

Brother C hasn't been asked to lead in prayer for two months and he thinks he's being slighted.

If the squabble concerns doctrine, the questions may not be exactly issues of primary importance. Such questions as "did John's disciples have to be rebaptized after Pentecost?" "Is it scriptural to say that a death angel passed over Egypt and took the first born?" "Where do the righteous dead go as they await the judgment?" and other similar issues can often lead to hard feelings and endless disputes. Quite often the doctrinal tests serve as a smoke screen to cover the jealousy and envy that really fuels the argument.

A new Christian who comes into that kind of atmosphere soon becomes discouraged and feels that he's crashed somebody else's party, unless he too is an issue-oriented person who has become a Christian merely because one set of arguments sounded better to him than another set.

A new Christian who enters this arena of combat steps unwittingly on all kinds of hidden mine fields and comes away feeling he's been used as a pawn in somebody else's war. Only the person who has the deepest sort of commitment coupled with a wholesome, mature outlook on life could be expected to survive in such a carnal atmosphere.

When inward congregational strife prevents incorporation, the only solution is genuine repentance. Brethren must know that their rude and divisive behavior provides an unbelieving world with an excuse to remain in its unbelief (John 17) and presents a stumbling block to those who are weak in faith (Romans 14). Congregational friction is an extremely serious matter. Paul counsels, "I appeal to you, brethren, to take note of those who create dissensions and difficulties in opposition to the doctrine which you have learned and avoid them" (Romans 16:17). Divided churches probably don't win many new members, and they will almost certainly drive away those new ones whom they do convert. Only those Christians who learn how to get along with one another can expect to save the lost and keep the saved in a saved condition. Consequently, good assimilation thinking requires us to prioritize the task of maintaining "the unity of the spirit in the bond of peace" (Ephesians 4:13).

Conclusion

If the church expects to incorporate its new members successfully, the church must concentrate on building a high-quality fellowship among its members, but that fellowship must be an open fellowship which makes it easy for new members to find acceptance.

Questions for Discussion

1. What is the Biblical meaning of "fellowship"?
2. What is the practical difference between fellowship and membership?
3. Discuss the similarities between the "membership-fellowship circle" concept proposed by Lyle Schaller and the "congregation" idea as perceived by C. Peter Wagner.
4. Why do the manipulative monologue techniques of soul winning hinder relationship building?
5. Why does the "teaching" approach often work against incorporation?
6. How might a nonmanipulative dialogue be employed in evangelism?
7. How valuable are campaigns to the total church growth objective?
8. Why do those who are converted in campaigns often drop out?
9. How can we make friendship evangelism effective?
10. How can we eliminate church conflict as a hindrance to incorporation?

Endnotes

[1]W. E. Vine, *Expository Dictionary of New Testament Words* (Old Tappan, New Jersey: Fleming H. Revell Company, 1966), p. 216.

[2]Lyle E. Schaller, *Assimilating New Members* (Nashville, Tennessee: Abingdon Press, 1979), p. 69.

[3]C. Peter Wagner, *Your Church Can Grow* (Ventura, California: Regal Books, 1980), p. 101.

[4]Flavil R. Yeakley, Jr., *Why Churches Grow* (Broken Arrow, Oklahoma: Christian Communications, Inc., 1979), p. 57.

[5]*Ibid.*, p. 58.

[6]*Ibid.*

[7]Win and Charles Arn, *The Master's Plan for Making Disciples* (Pasadena, California: Church Growth Press, 1982), p. 145. Win and Charles Arn are not members of the Church of Christ. Their terminology reflects their own faith commitments. It differs somewhat from the terminology in common use among the Churches of Christ.

[8]John R. W. Stott, "The Nature of Biblical Evangelism," in *World Vision*, October, 1974, pp. 12-13.

[9]Yeakley, *Why Churches Grow*, p. 66.

[10]John Naisbitt, *Megatrends* (New York: Warner Brothers Books, 1982), p. 233.

[11]Donald McGavran and George Hunter III, *Church Growth Strategies That Work* (Nashville, Tennessee: Abingdon Press, 1980), p. 30.

Chapter Seven

Does Your Congregation Extend Friendship?

Restoration-minded people have long emphasized the importance of preaching a pure gospel. Paul echoes this same thesis in Romans 1:16 when he boldly informs the church at Rome, "For I am not ashamed of the gospel; it is the power of God for salvation to everyone who has faith, to the Jew first and also to the Greek." In the same letter, he underscores the necessity of delivering that life-changing message through human instruments: "But how are men to call on him in whom they have not believed? And how are they to believe in him of whom they have not heard and how are they to hear without a preacher?" (Romans 10:14).

Quite often, Christians have assumed that any honest, seeking non-Christian who hears the Word proclaimed will inevitably believe the truth and obey the gospel. Christians also assume that non-Christians who decline the opportunity to become members of God's family have closed their minds to the reception of the truth. In addition to these two unwritten "laws of evangelism," some have added a third premise concerning the baptized person who falls away. Either the new convert is to be classified among those who "went out from us; but were not of us" like those John wrote about in 1 John 2:19; or they are like those whom Jesus mentioned in the parable of the sower: "the cares of the world and the delight in riches choke the word and it proves unfruitful" (Matthew 13:22).

Some of those who reject the gospel do indeed resist the truth. It's also true that many dropouts are more in love with the world than they are with Christ. But it's a mistake to assume that all those whom we fail to reach are insincere. It's also wrong to suppose that all those who leave us were either deceivers or lovers of this present world. Responsible stewardship of the gospel requires that we learn how to form caring relationships with people and that we continue sharing the information they need to hear. If we ignore the opportunity to build friendships with people, we're going to find ourselves shouting the gospel to empty pews, and we're going to continue to remain frustrated because people "can't stand the truth."

Friendship, An Essential Evangelistic Element

The American Institute for Church Growth in Pasadena, California, asked more than fourteen thousand church members this question: "What or who was responsible for your coming to Christ and the church?" When the results were tabulated, the institute identified eight reasons that people become identified with churches. Here are the results of that survey:

special need	1-2%
walk in	2-3%
minister	5-6%
visitation	1-2%
Sunday school	4-5%
crusades*	¼ of 1%
church programs	2-3%
friends/relatives	75-90%[1]

*Denotes campaigns and gospel meetings in Restoration terminology

The research being done in the church growth movement clearly demonstrates the correlation between friendship and a person's initial favorable contact with a church body. The research is just as conclusive concerning the importance of maintaining friendship after conversion. Consider the following observation from Charles and Win Arn:

> If after six months, the new member can identify few or no close friends who are active in the church, the chances are extremely high that the person will soon become inactive. But if the new member has a growing number of friends who are active in the church, it will be very unusual for that person to drop out. The "friendship factor" research is the most important element in whether a person remains active in a local church or drops out.[2]

The research conducted by Flavil R. Yeakley, Jr., in his doctoral dissertation at the University of Indiana, is often cited by writers in the church growth movement as evidence of the importance of friendship in keeping new members active in the church. Significantly, Dr. Yeakley's research was conducted among the Churches of Christ. As noted on page 32 of this work, Dr. Yeakley discovered that when people formed fewer than three friendships in the church within the first year of conversion, they inevitably dropped out. The converse is also true. If they formed more than seven new friendships, they inevitably stayed. The researcher concluded, "When a person has no meaningful personal contact with the congregation in the process of his conversion, he is likely to feel no meaningful sense of identification with his congregation after conversion and is therefore likely to drop out."[3]

What Is Friendship?

Since friendship is so vital to the incorporation process, we must be certain that we understand the nature of friendship. A casual acquaintance is not a friendship. Being able to call a person's name may be a start in the right direction, but it's not a guarantee that friendship formation is being generated. The Bible helps us to get started in our quest for friendship when it speaks of a "friend who sticks closer than a brother" (Proverbs 18:24). First Samuel 18:3 describes the depth of Jonathan's love for David: "He loved him as his own soul." Jesus challenged his disciples to a deepening friendship bond when he said, "You are my friends if you do what I command you" (John 15:14).

A study of the gospel accounts indicates that a close bond of friendship existed between Jesus and the twelve. A closer intimacy developed between Jesus, Peter, James, and John. Jesus also shared special ties with Mary, Martha, and Lazarus, who were outside the circle of the chosen twelve.

The apostle Paul needed friendship when he was coming to the end of life, so he wrote Timothy and pleaded with him to "do your best to come before winter" (2 Timothy 4:21). He felt abandoned by Demas, a man whom he had once described as beloved, but he was also comforted by the abiding friendship of Luke (2 Timothy 4:10-11). From all these Biblical accounts of friendship we can develop a partial list of vital friendship qualities:

1. Friendship involves personal intimacy.

2. Friendship is built on trust.

3. Friendship enables one to be transparent when in the company of those who have proven themselves to be true friends.

4. Friendship allows one to feel free to call for help in time of legitimate need.

5. Friendship means that one is willing to risk his own personal safety and comfort to meet the needs of his friends.

No wonder true friendship attracts more people to the church than any other human factor. The social critics of our times have described the current era as an age of alienation. We live in a world that has grown increasingly impersonal. The hostility level continues to rise, and most people are suspicious of those who say they want to be friendly. A certain cynicism develops because people have been burned too many times by hucksters and con artists. Yet, even in this cynical atmosphere, when hurting people realize they are being offered genuine friendship, they are drawn to it like insects are drawn to an electric light on a hot summer night.

Alan Loy McGinnis, a psychologist in Glendale, California, shares some encouraging thoughts concerning our ability to build relationships in his book, *The Friendship Factor:*

> In years of counseling, I have never met a person permanently disabled for love. It is possible that you have developed some rough edges which complicate your relationship and get you into trouble, but at the core you are fully capable of loving and being loved.[4]

Requirements of Effective Friendship

Very few people will take issue with the premise that strong churches are built on strong friendship patterns. However, church members sometimes either aren't aware of the requirements of friendship or they are unwilling to pay the price required for genuine bonding. Listed below are some requirements for developing friendships within a congregation.

1. *Church leaders must be willing to model friendship.* Many congregations have developed an unwritten policy against friendships being cultivated between church leaders and

other members of the local church. These policies are patterned more after the practice of American business and industry than the teachings of the New Testament. An elder in a certain congregation was explaining his reasons for believing that the elders shouldn't get too involved on a personal basis with other church members. He said, "Where I work, management personnel and the people who work on the line don't socialize. You never see line workers drinking coffee with their bosses." While his portrayal of how things usually function in the world of work is probably accurate, church leaders must realize they are leading the Lord's body. They are not running a human enterprise. It's not the purpose of this book to deal with labor and management relations in the contemporary commercial world. There are probably situations where an autocratic approach to leadership works quite efficiently. We must recognize, however, that we function under the authority of King Jesus, and you learn his system from the Bible, not by studying current business theory. The idea that a church leader should have no friends within the body simply won't square with scripture.

In John 10, Jesus describes himself as a shepherd. His analogies to leadership compare to the practices of a first-century Palestinian shepherd. Several of his statements indicate that the ancient shepherds maintained an intimate relationship with their sheep. In verse 3 he indicates that the sheep know his voice. The ancient shepherds each employed a unique sound which the sheep instantly recognized. When they were penned with other sheep, they would separate themselves from the larger flock and come running to the shepherd when they heard his call. Besides that, the shepherds gave the sheep names, and Jesus suggests that good shepherds know the names of every sheep. The sheep trust the shepherd so implicitly that they follow him wherever he leads them (verses 4 and 5). The shepherd's commitment to the sheep is so complete that he lays down his life for them (verse 11).

The other motif which describes the leadership style of

Jesus is that of a servant. In Mark 10:45, Jesus said, "For the son of man came not to be served, but to serve and to give his life as a ransom for many." When he washed the disciples' feet, he fleshed out this theory into actual practice (John 13). He even made their willingness to respond to this kind of service a requirement of sharing friendship with him (John 13:8).

In view of both the example and the explicit teaching of our Lord, does it not stand to reason that elders, deacons, preachers, and other church leaders not only have the privilege of forming friendships in the local church, but must actually take the lead in doing so in order that others may learn from their example? How can members of the church ever learn how to build relationships if they never see them modeled by their leaders?

Of course, leaders must be careful to avoid favoritism, nepotism, exclusivism, and all those negative forms of relating which would dehumanize and discriminate against those who are being led. The worth of people must be affirmed at all costs, but developing close relationships with people doesn't necessarily mean that one is practicing discrimination. After all, our Lord was closer to John than he was to Peter, but he never treated Peter as if he were a person of lesser value. Furthermore, there is no evidence that Peter ever became jealous of John.

2. *Friendships must be unconditional.* People very soon understand that friendship is less than genuine if our words and our behavior suggest "I'll love you when..." or "I'll love you until...." Many new Christians protect hidden skeletons in their closets—memories from the past that they would rather forget. Such skeletons may include a premarital pregnancy, a drinking problem, an orientation toward homosexuality, a drug history, a prison record, and the list goes on. Many people who seek Christ and the church are trying to find healing for some kind of inward pain. Only a few people who seek our fellowship already have their heads on straight morally and are simply opting for what they believe to be a stronger set of doctrinal premises. The

new people who come into the body are usually recovering from wounds inflicted by the devil. The wounds are all on the inside, so they aren't apparent to us by anything we see on the outside. These new brethren who have been morally scarred by their past look much like all the other Christians in the fellowship. They show up at the worship service wearing Hart, Shafner and Marx suits, and their wives wear dresses from Nieman-Marcus. They greet other members with radiant smiles and talk about what's playing at Cinema 4. When they're invited into a church member's home, they compliment the roast beef and apple pie. They enthusiastically talk about the sermon, the song service, and even the topics covered in Bible class.

Christians who have managed to avoid the seamier forms of sin sometimes go into shock when they learn about a new Christian's sordid past. Sometimes we don't realize that such people still carry quite a lot of emotional baggage from their past lives. One may even realize that he's been washed clean by the blood of the Lamb, but he still has a need to work through the emotional damage that sin has inflicted on his personality. It's quite possible that such a person will find therapeutic value in being able to verbalize some of his past problems in the presence of another brother or sister. He may risk sharing his past problems, his present struggles, and his fears about the future with a person whom he perceives to be a more mature Christian, in the hope that he can find understanding. When he decides to do so, he's testing the genuineness of that friendship.

If the older Christian turns out to be a fair-weather friend, the future growth of the new Christian may be jeopardized. Some Christians would like to think that life never gets any more complicated than the plot of a Shirley Temple movie. When they learn that the new Christian's struggle resembles *Peyton Place*, they decide the problem is too heavy, too complicated, and too hot to handle. Unfortunately, the Christian who realizes he's into a relationship that's over his head rarely comes right out and says, "Brother, I love you dearly, but I've never had to deal with the kinds of problems you've faced in your life. I may not be very helpful, so why don't you talk to Sam Jones? His story sounds a lot like yours, and he's doing well in his walk with the Lord." Instead, the older Christian most often unilaterally terminates the relationship. He stops giving out invitations to dinner. He avoids talking with the "tainted" brother or sister at service times. If he's forced into a conversation, he makes sure the topic never gets beyond the weather and "how are you feeling today?" Worst of all, he withdraws the expressions of caring and helping. He simply treats the new Christian as a nonperson. That's conditional friendship. Most people see through that kind of fair-weather treatment, and many leave the church in disillusionment.

We need to remember that the early church was able to extend friendship to people like Paul who had a murderous past, to a little girl in Philippi who once had been demon-possessed, and even to a Corinthian brother who once practiced incest. The Colossian church included many people with shameful personal histories. Their behavior pattern included "fornication, impurity, passion, evil desire and covetousness" (Colossians 3:5). When Paul mentioned these pre-Christian sins, he reminded the brothers and sisters, "In these you once walked, when you lived in them" (Colossians 3:7). The New Testament record is clear. God expects us to extend unconditional friendship to people whose past lives have not always been admirable.

3. *Friendship must be nonmanipulative.* Some years ago, I called on an elderly couple in an attempt to secure an appointment for a Bible study. They readily granted the appointment. I soon learned that they had moved into our area from another part of the country. They had no real friends. When I offered to study the Bible with them, they were quite receptive and readily cooperated in the first study. As we concluded that study, they told me their previous experience with Bible study. A lady from the church had come to their home and had presented a set of filmstrips about the Bible. At the conclusion of the series. she had asked them to consider being baptized. They declined.

They said, "She was a very nice lady and we enjoyed visiting with her so much, but when we decided not to be baptized, she never came back, and we were very disappointed." To my own shame, I never went back either.

Perhaps the lady who showed the filmstrip was thinking about the Lord's instruction to the seventy when he said, "But whenever you enter a town and they do not receive you, go into the streets and say 'even the dust of your town clings to our feet, we wipe off against you; nevertheless know this that the kingdom of God has come near'" (Luke 10:10-11). Before we invoke that passage, we need to understand that the circumstances and guidelines which governed the seventy aren't the principles that control our behavior in evangelistic outreach today. For one thing, they went out two by two. They went only to the lost sheep of the house of Israel. They didn't even take money or a change of clothes when they went out. Their ministry was limited in its scope, in its message, and in the time the message was to be proclaimed. The gospel we preach is not subject to those limitations. While it's true that we're stewards of our time and it's also true that there's a certain urgency connected with proclaiming the message, there's something obscene about forming friendships and then dropping them like a hot potato to run in pursuit of a better prospect.

If we go back to the shepherd motif in John 10 as a pattern for relationship building, it's clear that the hireling is the one who forms relationships for what he can get out of them. According to Jesus, the hireling bails out of his responsibility when danger threatens or when his wages are cut off. The true shepherd doesn't forget about the sheep when the little lamb strays away from the flock. He doesn't disown a lamb when it comes into the sheep pen with cuts and bruises. The sheep trust the shepherd because he remains their friend through storms, disease, and every other kind of problem that complicates their lives.

Many people are suspicious of church members because they believe Christians behave more like hirelings than shepherds. The secular person thinks every interest of the church is tied to the offering plate. The only way that impression can be corrected is through the offering of long-term, unconditional, nonmanipulative friendship. Such relationships can be quite costly.

> Deep friendship requires cultivation over the years—evenings before the fire, long walks together and lots of time to talk. It requires keeping the television off, so the two of you can log in with each other. If your social calendar is too full to provide intimate bonding, it should be pared.[5]

4. *Friendships must be reciprocal.* Sometimes an incorporation-conscious Christian may genuinely desire to extend friendship, but the other person is unwilling to receive it. Hosea deeply loved his wife, Gomer. Sadly, Gomer never returned Hosea's unconditional love. Hosea's home life served as an object lesson to teach the nation of Israel of God's patient love, but Hosea's home was never really a happy home.

There are some people who either cannot or will not respond to our friendship overtures. Perhaps their past experiences have been so painful they can't bring themselves to trust in people. Sometimes the socioeconomic distance between two people is simply a chasm that's too wide to bridge. As one reads the letter to Philemon, there's every reason to believe that Philemon has responded to Paul's plea to accept Onesimus, his runaway slave as a brother. But did they ever become close friends? Did Philemon and Onesimus sit on the back porch in the cool of the afternoon and share small talk with each other? Did they tell one another jokes, or share their opinions on Roman politics? I doubt it. Socioeconomic differences put them in two different worlds.

Age can prevent the development of reciprocal friendships. While cross-generational respect does frequently occur, it's the exception rather than the rule when a 42-year-old business executive becomes a close friend with an

18-year-old high school senior. The high school senior likes cars with mag wheels and prefers music by Michael Jackson. The business executive drives a conservative-looking Olds 98 and prefers music by Henry Mancini.

Temperamental differences can make friendship difficult. Some people are loud and demonstrative, while others are quiet and reserved. I have a friend who talks with such tremendous volume that he can tell a joke in a crowded restaurant and people who are sitting two or three tables away will laugh at the punch line. Some people think he's a neat fellow because he's uninhibited. Others try to avoid being in the same restaurant with him. His behavior is neither right nor wrong. His loudness is simply part of his personality. The fact that he's my friend probably says something about my own volume level. On the other hand, he doesn't attract too many introverted friends.

Conclusion

Flavil Yeakley sums up the kind of relationship development that must take place within our fellowship if we expect our outreach ministries to achieve lasting results:

> When a personal worker comes into a subject's house carrying a projector, screen, records, charts and other aids for a cottage meeting, that is what many people in the church of Christ call personal evangelism. However, the subjects exposed to this kind of evangelism did not see it as very personal at all. They saw such persons as equipment manipulators. Results seemed to be better when the tool was simply an open Bible. And yet it is not really as simple as that. What is important is the *quality of the relationship,* not the structure of the teaching method used nor the kinds of tools that are used.[6]

If the quality of the relationship is important in the process of persuading someone to become a Christian, then the value of building quality relationships certainly increases as new members develop a sense of belonging.

Questions for Discussion

1. Why is it necessary to combine relationship building with sound gospel teaching to make and keep Christians?
2. Why do 75 to 90 percent of those who become church members do so as the result of the influence of friends and relatives?
3. How would you describe a friend?
4. How many friendships can one person expect to realistically maintain?
5. Why are some people attracted to the offer of genuine friendship?
6. Why are some people suspicious of the way most church people offer to extend friendship?
7. What are the pros and cons of church leaders having close friends?
8. What is meant by unconditional friendship?
9. What traits should we look for in others when we are trying to make friends?
10. List some ways that people tend to make friendships manipulative.

Endnotes

1Win and Charles Arn, *The Master's Plan for Making Disciples* (Pasadena, California: Church Growth Press, 1982), p. 148.

2*Ibid.*

3Flavil R. Yeakley, *Why Churches Grow,* 3rd ed. (Broken Arrow, Oklahoma: Christian Communications, Inc., 1979), p. 66.

4Alan Loy McGinnis, *The Friendship Factor* (Minneapolis, Minnesota: Augsburg Publishing House, 1979), p. 188.

5*Ibid.*, p. 24.

6Yeakley, *Why Churches Grow,* p. 17.

Chapter Eight

Love One Another—
The Nuts and Bolts
of Relationship Building

Jesus placed a premium on relationship building when he said, "A new commandment I give to you. Love one another; even as I have loved you, that you also love one another. By this shall all men know that you are my disciples if you have love for one another" (John 13:34-35). From this we understand that we establish credibility for our faith through building strong relationships within the body. The people of the world can easily turn off our radio and television broadcasts. They can throw our literature into their garbage cans. They usually avoid attending our services even when we mount massive campaigns and spend thousands of dollars for expensive advertising. They can easily say, "No, thank you," when we approach them for Bible studies. There's one thing, however, which the world cannot ignore. That one thing is the supportive love which true Christians demonstrate toward one another.

While our Lord's new commandment is easily understood, putting it into practice through the performance of loving attitudes and actions requires discipline. Some people are hard to love. Their lives and their thought patterns have been so twisted and warped by negative value systems that love can't penetrate their defense mechanisms without tremendous effort on our part. Besides that, we have some problems getting ourselves geared up to engage in loving actions. Some of us have lived so long with our own self-centeredness that it's extremely painful to abandon our self-interests and lay down our lives for somebody else, especially when we're not sure that the person who requires our attention is worth it.

Loving comes more easily for some people. Every congregation has members who had the advantage of growing up in caring families where affirmation, warmth, affection, touching, and serving were all a part of the family life style. These people have a head start in practicing the kind of love that helps new Christians develop a sense of belonging.

Some in the church aren't really people-oriented. We have those who are thing-oriented, those who are doctrine-oriented, those who are issue-oriented, and those who are task-oriented. While all these concerns are important, it's necessary for members of the Lord's church to learn that we're first and foremost in the people business. That's the implication of the new commandment.

Some would like to be people-oriented, but they're shy and introverted. Some are insecure and fear rejection when they offer friendship. Some don't know how to carry on a conversation, and some are afraid of being hurt because of past experiences in relationship building. If you're among those who lack confidence in your ability to build relationships, this chapter is for you. There's no such thing as a Christian who can't learn how to relate to people. Jesus would never have given this new commandment if it were impossible to obey. I'm not suggesting that every Christian has to become a gregarious, back-slapping extrovert. There are many different ways to show love, and even shy people can learn to do it. To borrow a line from an old television show, "different folks need different strokes." Relationship building skills do require discipline, and learning the techniques of friendship development isn't always an easy task. Rest assured that you can become a lover of people if you persevere through the ups and downs of the loving process. The rest of this chapter will focus on some of the nuts and bolts of practicing love within the Lord's body.

Narrow Your Focus

It's unrealistic to think that you can love everyone in the church with equal intensity. Jesus didn't do it. The apostles didn't do it. And neither should we try to spread ourselves so thin that we become dabblers in the commodity of love. We must learn to narrow the focus, but how do we go about it? McGinnis is right on target when he says, "The fact of the matter is that we cannot have a profound connection with more than a few people. Time prohibits it."[1] As a means of determining which ones you can realistically touch with your life, you might ask the following questions:

*How close are we in age?

*What are his/her family responsibilities, and what are mine?

*What is his socioeconomic status in relation to mine?

*What intellectual interests do we have in common?

*What views do we share?

*What are his/her understandings and misunderstandings with regard to the faith, and how well am I equipped to deal with the misunderstandings?

*What problems has he/she faced? Have I ever faced a similar problem?

*What social and recreational interests do we share?

By asking such questions, you can begin to construct a list of persons with whom you may potentially develop significant relationships. One word of caution is in order, however. We must make sure that all new Christians have friends. If you can't realistically form a friendship with a certain new Christian, your contribution to assimilation may be that of getting him together with someone who has the right combination of personality and skills to help him grow.

There will also be times when our common interest in Christ so far overshadows all other considerations that we will be able to build a close bond even when we appear to be running down different tracks in all other areas. For this reason, don't be too hasty in ruling out a potential friendship because of age differences, cultural differences, interest differences, etc.

Build Relationships Through Caring Acts

1. *Start out with burden bearing.* "Bear one another's burden and so fulfill the law of Christ" (Galatians 6:2). Paul's admonition to the Galatians extends the command of John 13:34-35 into the arena of daily living. Robert Schuller's famous slogan, "Find a need and fill it; find a hurt and heal it," is nothing more than a clever way of rewording Paul's statement in Galatians 6:2.

When I was a student in college, a missionary who had spent most of his life in Africa talked to a group of us about Christian service. He read from Matthew 25:42-26: ""for I was hungry and you gave me no food. I was thirsty and you gave me no drink. I was a stranger and you did not welcome me, naked and you did not clothe me, sick and in prison and you did not visit me.' Then they will also answer, "Lord, when did we see thee hungry or thirsty or a stranger or naked or sick or in prison and did not minister to thee?' Then will he answer them, 'Truly, I say to you, as you did it not unto one of the least of these you did it not to me. And these will go away into eternal punishment, but the righteous into eternal life.'" After he read those words, the missionary said, "Young people your destiny depends on your response to those needs." He might have added that the destiny of those new members who come into your fellowship may also depend on your response to the challenge of Matthew 25.

It's important to be available for hurting—when someone loses a loved one, goes through a serious illness, struggles with a rebellious child, fails in business or goes through the various kinds of trauma that make life oppressive. People are often most open to forming new relationships when they're down. When other friends are making themselves scarce, a hurting person may well respond to the offer of a genuine, caring Christian when his natural inclination at other times would be to decline such offers of friendship.

If you've passed through similar kinds of trauma yourself, you can help ease another person's burden simply by letting him know that you have passed this way. Perhaps you can even share how your faith and your continued service to God have sustained you when the hour seemed darkest.

About ten years ago, my wife and I passed through a severe marital crisis. It was probably the most painful experience of our entire lives. We had one thing going for us during that time. Because we had been brought up to respect the teachings of the Bible, we believed in the permanence of marriage. At one point, that was about all that held the marriage together. We knew that divorce could jeopardize our salvation. We decided to remain together at all costs. On the other hand, neither one of us wanted to spend the rest of our lives in a miserable relationship without communication and affection, so we set out to try to enrich our marriage. We picked up the pieces that were left and slowly started building the kind of bond we should have worked on in the beginning years of our marriage. The results were worth the struggle. Today, our relationship is strong. We enjoy an intimacy we had never before dreamed possible.

One of the by-products of our successful recovery has been our ability to minister to others who have experienced similar marital difficulties. We don't manage to help everybody we try to help, but we do help enough people to realize great satisfaction in knowing that our own experiences are beneficial to others. In the process, we've also formed some significant relationship that we probably wouldn't have cultivated had we not passed through our own valley of marital conflict.

Of course, if you're twenty-one years old and you've never experienced very many hard blows in life, you can't walk up to someone and say, "I've gone through something similar to what's happening in your life right now." Still, this doesn't mean that you can't be available for hurting. When I was twenty-two years old, I was ministering to grief at funerals. I was green as the grass on the lawn of a perpetual care cemetery, but I still made the effort, and some people even said it helped. You can find a way of letting people know you care, and you can be genuinely helpful even if that help consists of nothing more than making them aware of other resources.

2. *Learn to listen.* Attentive listening is one of the most difficult skills to acquire. We think faster than most people speak, and our minds tend to run way ahead of what a person wants to tell us. Some of us are afflicted with the compulsion to talk, so we spend most of our time trying to decide what we're going to say, rather than listening to what the other person is trying to tell us. If we can overcome these common deterrents to listening, we'll be way ahead of most of the rest of the world, and we can sometimes work wonders in the lives of other people.

Most of us need to heed the counsel of James: "Know this my beloved brethren. Let every man be quick to hear, slow to speak..."(James 1:10). Unfortunately, many of us specialize in reversing the process. The person who takes James seriously will most certainly find himself neck deep in people who want to become his friends.

> Since so few people genuinely attend to others, those who will learn to draw out the other person can be guaranteed all the friendship they can handle and be assured of deepening the relationships they presently own.[2]

108

In the Christian context, we sometimes have a hard time listening because we want to control the agenda of the conversation. We want to turn every conversation to the Word of God at the earliest opportunity. This often backfires because the other person gets the idea that we're not listening to him. You have your own idea about where the conversation ought to go, so you only pretend to listen to him in order to claim your equal-time rights.

> Attentive listening has no hidden agenda. Listening is not geared toward turning the conversation to spiritual matters at the first opportunity. Rather attentive listening seeks to understand...[a person's] dreams and ambitions; to discover his needs and his problems; and to develop a level of understanding that builds a mutual respect and personal empathy.[3]

3. *Spend quality time together.* It seems that we are always looking for shortcuts in ministry. We would really prefer that all our evangelistic experiences follow the model of Philip and the Ethiopian eunuch. We especially like the part which says, "The Spirit of the Lord caught up Philip; and the eunuch saw him no more and went on his way rejoicing" (Acts 8:39). Wouldn't it be wonderful if all the new Christians we reach would go on their way rejoicing? Then we could either go find someone else to share the gospel with or resume playing golf with our lifelong cronies.

Perhaps legitimate Philip-and-the-eunuch types of conversions do take place today on airplanes, in laundromats, in bus terminals, and at other locations where strangers meet, but these are surely exceptions to the general rule. Joseph C. Aldrich contends that "the proclamational dimension of evangelism seldom takes place in a vacuum."[4] He argues for an "incarnational/relational" approach to evangelistic outreach.[5] The key word in Aldrich's incarnational/relational premise is the term *presence.* Presence involves love, unity, good works, hope, social intimacy, acceptance, and understanding.[6] We demonstrate presence by spending time—quality time and lots of it—with those whom we seek to influence. It doesn't take the place of teaching, but it makes the teaching sound authentic to the ears of a new Christian. It involves implementing Paul's principles of becoming all things to all men (1 Corinthians 9:21).

This means that we will invest huge blocks of time with one person both before and after his conversion to Christ. We need to share all kinds of experiences. Nothing draws people together more effectively than sharing food. In the world of business and labor, people who are at odds with one another don't go out to lunch together. When people have someone over to their houses for meals, they don't invite enemies. Meal times are reserved for the company of friends. Sharing table fellowship with a new Christian is one of the fastest ways to cement a good relationship.

Recreation times, social gatherings, and entertainment events can also be shared with new Christians. One brother recalled his first year as a Christian. An elder came by his house every Friday evening during the fall to ask if he would like to attend the local high school football games. The new brother later said, "His thoughtfulness convinced me that I really belonged to the church."

Work provides another opportunity for activating love. From time to time we all have work tasks around the house and yard which require the effort of more than one person. There's no better way to strengthen a person's sense of belonging than to offer your skills, your time, and your sweat. He may need help pouring concrete, overhauling his car engine, or putting a new roof on his house. When you offer to help a new brother in some physical task, it's important not to over estimate your own abilities. It's possible to be more of a hindrance than a help.

4. *Capitalize on teachable moments.* If you spend enough quality time with a growing new Christian, the opportunity for teaching will inevitably arise, provided you are perceptive enough to recognize it. Perhaps you'll attend a school music concert together and on the way home, the new

Christian will say, "I've been wondering about something. I really don't understand why we don't have instrumental music in our services." That's a teachable moment. It's not a time to say, "I can't believe you've been in the church for six months and still don't understand the nature of New Testament authority." Instead, it's a time to patiently give the reasons why we choose to sing without the aid of instrumental music. You'll probably do more good than the preacher will if he delivers a dozen sermons on what's wrong with instrumental music.

Teachable moments come up in all kinds of places and situations. Several years ago, I went fishing with a new Christian. The fish didn't seem to be interested in the bait we offered them, so we mostly sat in the boat and talked. Suddenly, he reached into his pocket and pulled out a pack of cigarettes. He said, "Talk to me about these things." He knew about the surgeon general's report, and he had observed that most of his fellow church members didn't smoke. No one had backed him into a corner with remarks like, "When are you going to throw those filthy things away?" I just went through some reasons why I choose not to smoke. The whole thing was low key and nonthreatening. In a few days he gave up the habit. That teachable moment enabled me to be far more effective than I might have been had I thundered at him from the pulpit or tried to back him into a corner with unanswerable arguments.

Teachable moments aren't always easy to recognize. Sometimes they present themselves in far more subtle forms. Philip was able to recognize his teachable moment because (1) the eunuch was reading his Bible, (2) he was admittedly confused about what he was reading, and (3) he asked Philip a specific hermeneutical question (Acts 8:29-34). Paul recognized a teachable moment when the Philippian jailer became so distraught over the turn of events in his jail that he was ready to commit suicide (Acts 16). Some guidelines which can help us recognize teachable moments include the following:

*Teachable moments occur when questions are asked.

*Teachable moments occur when confusion is evident.

*Teachable moments are evident when spiritual interest is indicated.

*Teachable moments may be indicated by the presence of open Bibles on a coffee table, sermon tapes on a tape machine, tracts and books left lying open, and other evidence of personal study.

*Teachable moments are obvious when a person admits that he has needs and doesn't know where to turn for solutions to his problems.

*Teachable moments occur when a comment is made about a sermon, a spiritual book, or a spiritual idea.

*Teachable moments may be indicated when a person expresses concern over moral issues.

5. *Learn to communicate nonverbally.* Much of the closeness which develops between Christians grows because positive nonverbal signals are being sent and received. Some students of human behavior believe that more than ninety per cent of the messages sent and received by people are communicated nonverbally.

Nonverbal communication includes things like the tone of voice, the way one sits, a scowl or a smile on one's face, a yawn, a wink, eye contact, a hug, a handshake, and many other unspoken signals. Sometimes nonverbal communication cancels out the force of the words that are spoken. You've probably known someone who can say, "Good morning," and make a whole room full of people angry because he says it with a nasty tone of voice.

The Scriptures recognize the importance of nonverbal communication. According to Proverbs, "A *soft* answer turns away wrath" (Proverbs 15:1). Solomon mentions in Proverbs 6:17-18 seven things that God hates. The first one is a proud look (AV).

The Bible also addresses the subject of touching. Many

people are afraid to touch others for fear their intentions will be misread or for fear that touching can lead to a compromise of one's sexual ethics. The person who touches will be misunderstood sooner or later, but that's no reason to stop touching. Words are often misunderstood, and we don't use this fact as an excuse to stop talking. Some touching does have sexual overtones, and Christians would be well advised to be cautious in those areas.

The benefits of touching are much too positive to allow the dangers or the criticism to hinder us. We have ample Biblical precedent for affirmation through touching. When Jesus came into the room where Peter's mother-in-law was suffering from a fever, he touched her hand (Matthew 8:15). When little children were brought to Jesus, "he took them in his arms and blessed them" (Mark 10:16). At the meeting in the upper room before the crucifixion, John reports that he was "lying close to the breast of Jesus" (John 13:23). The early Christians regularly greeted one another with a "holy kiss" (Romans 16:16). The practice of Jesus and the early church gives us ample precedent to engage in touching as a means of deepening the bonds of friendship.

> Our bodies can become our best tools for achieving genuine intimacy with those around us. If you observe those who have deep relationships you will find that although few of them are indiscriminate grabbers who hug everyone in sight, most have delicately tuned their sense of touch and it is in use every time they are with people.[7]

By suggesting that we strengthen relationships through touching, I'm not implying that Christians have to become gushers. Touching may be confined to a mere handshake in some instances. Many men find it very difficult to hug other men. Men kissing men is almost taboo in American society, although that's not true in other cultures. There's enough latitude in the way people can touch and be touched to fit the needs of everyone. The important thing to remember is that people need to be touched.

6. *Confrontation*. Confrontation is perhaps the most difficult part of relationship building. Nevertheless, there comes a time when it must be done. Paul says, "Brethren, if a man be overtaken in a trespass, you who are spiritual should restore him in the spirit of gentleness. Look to yourself, lest you too be tempted" (Galatians 6:1-2). James addresses the same need: "My brethren, if any one among you wanders from the truth and someone brings him back, let him know that whoever brings a sinner back from the error of his way will save a soul from death and will cover a multitude of sins" (James 5:19-20).

Many horror stories have been told concerning those who use the bull-in-a-China-closet technique of confrontation. I grew up in an atmosphere in which many church members advocated, "Preach the gospel and let the chips fall where they may." Occasionally, mean and spiteful things were said to people and justified on the basis that "the truth sometimes hurts." The truth does indeed hurt sometimes, but God forbid that we should ever be harsh and vindictive in the way we verbalize it. Paul says the erring brother should be confronted with gentleness.

Sometimes contemporary Christians withdraw from confronting because they don't want to fall into the trap of coming across as insensitive people. It helps to remember that we confront an erring brother because we love him too much to allow him to continue down a destructive path unchecked. If we decide to just let him alone, we may later regret not having done what we could when we had the opportunity. Em Griffin calls those people who want to live and let live, "non lovers."

> At first blush this looks like an attractive option, for the non lover avoids all the manipulative excesses entered into by the false lover...
>
> The detached stance, however, is a luxury unavailable to the Christian...to decide not to influence is to let others' influence hold sway.[8]

114

If we truly love, we will confront. Our confrontation will be more effective when we've first given attention to all the other caring acts. Most of us don't accept correction very well from people who have never taken the time to work at understanding us. At the same time, we must also remember that the person we're confronting has a free will and as much as it may disappoint us, he is free to reject our viewpoint.

Enlarge the New Christian's Circle of Friends

No Christian is broad enough in his total response to life to be able to meet all the relationship needs of another Christian. We don't serve the Lord in isolation, and we don't serve the Lord in pairs. The new Christian needs the fellowship of the body. Paul pictures the body functioning to "equip the saints for the work of ministry" (Ephesians 4:12). To complete the process of relationship building, we must help our new friends in Christ develop all the healthy associations they will need to grow in grace and knowledge. Our older friends in the faith possess gifts which will assist the new Christians in the maturation process. It takes all of us working together to make sure that our new brothers and sisters will not be "tossed to and fro carried about with every wind of doctrine, by the cunning of men, by their craftiness in deceitful wiles" (Ephesians 4:14).

Conclusion

Relationship building involves us in the sometimes pleasant, sometimes unpleasant business of loving both in word and in deed. There'll be times when we will lend a helping hand and somebody will slap it. There'll be other times when we'll do our best to say, "We care," and some people will misunderstand our intentions. There'll be times when our own spiritual attitudes are so poor that we'll temporarily lapse into nonloving behavior.

Through it all, we still have the ability to exercise choices.

We can withdraw and protect our own feelings, or we can pick ourselves up off the floor and go at it again. It's worth trying again and again because loving is the only way that ministry gets done, and obeying the new command is the only kind of life style that really satisfies.

Questions for Discussion

1. How does "loving one another" establish our credibility in the eyes of an unbelieving world?
2. Why is it important to narrow our focus when seeking out friendships?
3. What additional factors should a person consider when trying to determine which friendships he should cultivate?
4. List some of the situations in which a Christian can become involved in bearing the burdens of new Christians.
5. How can we become better listeners?
6. What is your definition of quality time?
7. How can we sharpen our perception of teachable moments?
8. What guidelines should govern the Christian in touching other people?
9. What is the best way to go about confronting someone who needs correction?
10. How can we do a more effective job of helping new Christians expand their friendship contacts with the body?

Endnotes

[1]Alan Loy McGinnis, *The Friendship Factor* (Minneapolis, Minnesota: Augsburg Publishing House, 1979), p. 24.

[2]Win and Charles Arn, *The Master's Plan for Making Disciples* (Pasadena, California: Church Growth Press, 1982), p. 88.

[3]*Ibid.*

[4]Joseph C. Aldrich, *Lifestyle Evangelism* (Portland, Oregon: Multnomah Press, 1981), p. 83.

[5]*Ibid.*, p. 81.

[6]*Ibid.*, p. 82.

[7]Alan Loy McGinnis, *The Friendship Factor,* p. 85.

[8]Em Griffin, *The Mindchangers* (Wheaton, Illinois: Tyndale House, 1976), p. 32.

Chapter Nine

A New Christian's Knowledge Needs

Christianity is a taught religion. Jesus said, "And you will know the truth and the truth will make you free" (John 8:32). When ancient Israel lapsed into apostasy, God used the lips of the prophets to inform them, "My people are destroyed for lack of knowledge" (Hosea 4:6). Our eternal destiny depends on our response to teaching. On another occasion, Jesus said, "If any one hears my sayings and does not keep them, I do not judge him; for I did not come to judge the world. He who rejects me and does not receive my sayings has a judge; the word that I have spoken will be his judge on the last day" (John 12:47-48).

Paul clearly understood that his failure to discern properly the teachings of the gospel caused him to react against the church in hostility. While admitting that he had once been a bitter antagonist to the church, he said, "I received mercy because I had acted ignorantly in unbelief" (1 Timothy 1:13). As he moved across Asia Minor and later into Europe, he used teaching as his behavior modification tool. The equipping gifts that were used to build up the body of Christ included prophecy, evangelism, and teaching

(Ephesians 4:11-16). Of the seven gifts to be employed in life transformation, three directly involve teaching—prophecy, teaching, and exhortation (Romans 12:3-8). It's significant that elders in the church are required to be proficient in teaching (1 Timothy 3:2).

Even when the miraculous gifts were being transmitted through the laying on of the apostle's hands, the dissemination of information through human instruments occupied a position of importance. One of the gifts was "the utterance of knowledge" (1 Corinthians 12:8). Although some people want to spotlight the tongues gift, the interpretation gift actually received greater prominence. Paul writes, "Now, brethren, if I come to you speaking in tongues, how shall I benefit unless I bring you some revelation or knowledge or prophecy or teaching?" (1 Corinthians 14:6).

In previous chapters, heavy stress was given to relationship building as a means of attracting people to Christ and keeping them in the body. If the balance of material between information transmission and relationship building seems disproportionate, it's because we seem to have understood the necessity of teaching more than we have understood the importance of loving. Nevertheless, we shouldn't be lulled into thinking that we can ignore teaching in favor of establishing relationships. If we build a caring community without giving attention to the saving message of Christ, we've done little more than establish a Christian service club with a Christian facade. Paul's language in 1 Corinthians 1:21 still applies: "For since in the wisdom of God, the world did not know God through wisdom, it pleased God through the folly of what we preach to save those who believe."

How Knowledge Is Communicated

Some people believe that learning takes place when beliefs, insights, convictions, and interpretations which have been formed in the mind of a teacher are then transferred without modification to the mind of a student. To carry this theory a step further, learning would result in a pupil's adoption of the same attitude and life style as that of the teacher. Those who adhere to this theory of learning like to point to the words of Jesus: "A disciple is not above his teacher; but every well trained student will be like his teacher" (Luke 6:40).

Without question, every Christian should want to be like Jesus. As a disciple of Christ, my goal in life is to become like the one who died for me. I'm not there yet and to be quite honest, I'm still working on certain aspects of my desire as well as my practice. I'm constantly challenged by the nobility of Paul's goal statement in Philippians 3:8, "Indeed, I count everything as loss because of the surpassing worth of knowing Christ Jesus my Lord." I can say, "Amen" to that statement without reservation. The hard part comes when I drop down a little further in the text and read his explanation of that goal statement. Paul wants to "know him and the power of his resurrection." I'm all for the power part, but he goes on to say that he wants to "share his sufferings, becoming like him in his death" (Philippians 3:11). That's where I balk. My desire hasn't matched up to Paul's desire yet, because I'm not really into suffering and dying.

Although I may still have some distance to go to follow the path of discipleship to its ultimate end, I have no trouble respecting Jesus as my discipler. I'm not so very excited about blindly following the leadership of some human being who says he wants to disciple me, however. I simply don't have that much confidence in mere men.

When we attempt to transmit information to people by reproducing our own thought patterns in their minds, we're playing an extremely dangerous game. We open ourselves up to the temptation to become manipulative and ego hungry. Some people justify this spiritual cloning technique by saying, "I'm just teaching what the Bible says. I take myself completely out of the picture by giving book, chapter and verse for everything I teach." Sounds noble, doesn't it? How can any fair person possibly take issue with the Bible?

The problem lies in our human frailties. Surely, God's Word is written in understandable language, and his message concerning salvation and Christian growth was never intended to be a message of confusion. Unfortunately, human beings are not immune to bias, stubbornness, traditionalism, and ignorance. Many of us tend to be judgmental and opinionated, whether we admit it or not. The best-trained Bible student among us has blind spots that he's unable to recognize. The Word itself isn't flawed, but the minds of men are, and that includes the minds of our own brethren. Neither Campbell, Stone, Lipscomb, Brewer, Wallace, nor any other scholar in our fellowship comprehended truth in such completeness that every position held can be swallowed hook, line, and sinker.

Some would-be disciplers seem to feel they have matured enough to take complete charge of developing another person's spiritual life. Not only does this create an unhealthy dependence on the part of the one being discipled, but the discipler is confronted with the temptation to take himself on the ultimate ego trip. He may even begin to think of himself as exhibit A in Christian living. Apparently this is one of the reasons the Holy Spirit warns against appointing newly won converts to the office of bishop. He runs the risk of becoming conceited and "falling into the condemnation of the devil" (1 Timothy 3:6).

A far healthier approach to informational transmission involves providing the new Christian with skills to conduct his own studies in an atmosphere of mutual respect and friendship. It will be remembered that Yeakley's studies showed that people are far more likely to remain active in the church if they perceive the study situation in which the gospel was presented as a nonmanipulative dialogue rather than as an information transmission experience or a manipulative monologue.

> The optimal situation is not one in which the subject sees the personal worker as being vastly superior in knowledge. In that situation, the subject is likely to feel intimidated. What is best is for the personal worker to be seen as knowing just a little more about the Bible than the subject does. [1]

Sometimes people feel intimidated by preachers who try to teach them. They feel they've been placed at a disadvantage because they're unable to match wits with such learned men. Consequently, they would rather study with someone who has a little less "polish."

Many commercially prepared materials have been designed to transmit information to the new Christian. Many, if not most of these materials are useful. However, some of them concentrate only on doctrinal information and fail to take into consideration the various emotional, spiritual, social, and intellectual dynamics that have been discussed in preceding chapters.

Areas of Study for the New Christian

Rather than recommend specific materials[2], the following suggestions will be made concerning study areas which will help Christians grow. It might be wise to begin a file of materials in these areas and then develop your own study course to fit your personality.

1. *Reinforcement of conversion.* If you've ever bought a new car and signed your name to a 48-month note, you may well have experienced a syndrome known as the "buyer's blues." The new Christian sometimes develops this same kind of feelings shortly after his conversion.

Many different influences may bring on these doubts. One source of doubt is the reaction of family members. Yeakley discovered,

> ". . .when there is a very homogeneous pattern of religious influence in a circle of friends and relatives, the person who is regarded as the religious opinion leader is more likely to convert than the low status member of that group. If such a leader converts, he is likely to bring the entire group with him.[3]

Yeakley also suggested that the converse is true. If a person converts whose opinion is not highly regarded by the family or group, research indicates a much higher incidence of reversion to one's original religious moorings or life style. Yeakley takes issue with those personal evangelism techniques which focus on single persons and nuclear families when the support group and the extended family basically adheres to the same religion. He contends that more effective results will occur if attention can be focused on that group's opinion leader.[4]

These observations would suggest that a person who comes into the church and finds himself at odds with his entire family or support group will face some terrific pressures. It's not uncommon for such persons to be told they've been trapped by a cult. If the family or support group includes persons trained in theology or people who regard themselves as experts in religion (even if they are poorly informed), the group will most certainly put forth a concerted effort to find flaws in the wayward group member's new religion.

The salvation issues, therefore, need to be restudied and reinforced. Perhaps the most effective method of reinforcement is to guide the new Christian into a self-study program of pertinent scriptures and then to be available to answer questions and offer help when it's needed.

If we can challenge new Christians to become independent Bible students, we can make more rapid progress in helping people become fruit-bearing members of the Lord's body. Our role will likely be far more effective if we see ourselves as facilitators and not as indoctrinators.

It's important for the new Christian to understand that he abides in Christ. His relationship to Christ is the source of his spiritual life. Jesus said, "Abide in me and I in you. As a branch cannot bear fruit by itself unless it abides in the vine, neither can you unless you abide in me" (John 15:4). Every fruit-bearing Christian must know how he came to abide in Christ and be able to pinpoint the exact time when he put aside the old way of life and started the new. Part of the informational need that a new Christian experiences is the need to increase his confidence concerning the validity of his new life.

2. *Handling temptation.* New Christians often come to Christ after years of engaging in life styles in which their decisions about life were undisciplined. Paul reminded the Ephesian Christians that they were once "dead through the trespasses and sins in which you once walked, following the course of this world, following the prince of the power of the air, the spirit that is now at work in the sons of disobedience" (Ephesians 2:2-3).

In the past, many of our evangelistic efforts have been aimed at people whose life style was already essentially Christian—good, moral people who happened to have Christian spouses, members of denominations whose doctrinal understandings we set out to change, people who had been reared in Christian homes but just never had got around to obeying the gospel.

In today's world, many of those who are most open to the gospel are more like those people whom Paul describes in Ephesians 2. Religious sociologists call them the "unchurched." In his book *Lifestyle Evangelism*, Joseph C. Aldrich indicts evangelical Christianity for developing an isolationist stance toward unchurched people. He writes, "I think it is fair to say that the majority of Christians have lost their ability to relate significantly to non-Christians."[5] Most of us feel a certain amount of tension when we're in the presence of "unchurched" secular people. We're offended by their smoking, their drinking, their use of language, their attitudes toward divorce, their views about morality, and numerous other practices which clash with our own set of values. It's understandable that we would gravitate toward those whose outward behavior conforms more to our own. Unfortunately, we fail to realize that the "unchurched" people may be more conscious of their need than those denominational people we've been trying to debate all these years. If we can look beyond the immediate and obvious tension points, we'll see that they experience many of the same kinds of needs that we do.

The new Christian is told he has "nothing in common" with his unsaved associates. Quite frankly, I have a lot in common with them: a mortgage, car payments, kids who misbehave, a lawn to mow, a car to wash, a less-than-perfect marriage, a few too many pounds around my waist, and an interest in sports, hobbies and other activities they enjoy. It is well to remember that Jesus was called a "friend of sinners."[6]

Those who have been willing to invest time in cultivating relationships with unchurched people have found that many of them are open to becoming Christians. It requires a willingness to work at understanding and great patience, but the actual teaching is often much easier than teaching a person who is committed to some form of religious error. Charles Mylander gives this encouraging report: "According to the number of adherents reported by the present congregations, more than 80 million people remain unchurched. Some are resistant, but many are winnable."[7] While it may sound somewhat discouraging to think about a majority of our people being basically unchurched, that statistic also presents a tremendous opportunity. Our restoration emphasis, paired with an undenominational understanding of the nature of the church, offers a healthy alternative to the millions of people who have grown sick of denominationalism.[8] We can view many of these unchurched people as winnable, honest souls who have not bowed the knee to denominationalism.

But what happens when a secularly oriented person becomes a Christian? Most are immediately confronted with a number of decisions to be made. Does his commitment to Christ mean giving up his live-in girl friend? What's he going to do about the drugs he's been using? And will he still bar hop with his friends on Saturday night? And just what does this "dying to self" principle mean? Does it mean staying home and painting the garage on Saturdays, as his wife has been nagging him to do, or can he go fishing, as he had been planning? Then there are decisions to make about things like smoking, drinking, language habits, and his general life style of undisciplined behavior. How's he going to tell his boss that he can no longer misrepresent the company's product to the consumer? Suddenly he's faced with problems which had never been problems before.

And what happens when he lapses into some of the old behavior patterns? We can be sure that lapses will occur. Paul makes it clear that "if any one is in Christ, he is a new creation; the old has passed away, behold the new has come" (2 Corinthians 5:21). Although conversion brings us into a new relationship with God, we still live in the old flesh, and that old flesh is vulnerable. The same apostle wrote, "I pommel my body and subdue it, lest after preaching to others, I myself should be disqualified" (1 Corinthians 9:27).

We must help our new brother to learn how to deal with those terrible moments when the flesh makes demands on him. When he loses that battle, we need to be there to reassure him that it's only a temporary setback and that his defeat doesn't invalidate his conversion.

Relationship building is important in helping new Christians through these rough times. Other chapters have focused on building unconditional caring relationships, but there are also some knowledge needs that require his attention. Truth not only frees people from error, it also frees them from the subtle message of Satan that would either retard or extinguish faith altogether. The new Christian must develop an awareness of his resources for dealing with temptation. While the devil is a master deceiver, the new Christian has access to a package of benefits which include the ability to escape temptation. "No temptation has overtaken you that is not common to man. God is faithful, and he will not let you be tempted beyond your strength, but with the temptation will also provide the way of escape, that you may be able to endure it" (1 Corinthians 10:13).

It's important for the new Christian to realize that the

127

promise of a way of escape is only a part of the package. He might reason this way: "The passage says I won't be tempted beyond my strength, but I don't really have all that much strength. After all my life was very undisciplined for a lot of years." At that point, he needs some additional information. As he studies the Book of Romans in general and the eighth chapter in particular, he will discover another treasure in his benefits package. That treasure is called the Holy Spirit. Paul says the person whose mind is set on the Spirit has life and peace (Romans 8:6). As the new Christian continues to contemplate the superlatives of Romans 8, he will come to realize that he doesn't have to rely on his own strength. He will discover a truly amazing portion of his benefits package in verse 13: ". . . but if by the Spirit, you put to death the deeds of the body you will live." He'll even discover that this powerful Spirit lives within him (Romans 8:11).

As the informational needs of the Christian are being fulfilled, he will realize that he has enough resources at his disposal to win when Satan decides to play hardball. Of course, there will be those lapses. There will be those times when he'll forget to use the resources in his benefits package. What does he do then? When we brought the new member to Christ, and did our job correctly, we told him about grace—the undeserved favor of God. If we don't do that, we really haven't taught the gospel at all. Those who teach only the conditions of salvation have saddled the new Christian with a set of legalistic requirements that won't serve them well when they've stumbled into sin.

One of the most remarkable benefits in the Christian's package of blessing is the promise recorded in 1 John 1:7: "If we walk in the light, as he is in the light, we have fellowship with one another, and the blood of Jesus his Son cleanses us from all sin." It's within the power of the Christian to walk outside the light of God's love if he so chooses, but he doesn't walk out of the light every time he sins. We don't bounce in and out of grace a dozen times a day. If we're still walking with Jesus, his blood keeps us clean.

3. *Prayer.* The key to a new Christian's growth is learning how to pray. Prayer also requires knowledge. The prayer life of the new Christian will be discussed in some detail in chapter 12.

4. *Dealing with false teachers.* If this were a perfect world, people would become Christians and would grow in Christ's likeness without hindering obstacles. Unfortunately, this is not a perfect world, and it seems that teachers of false doctrines often view one's conversion to Christ as an opportunity to challenge the new Christian's faith. A loving Christian must protect the new Christian when he is in a vulnerable position. Quite often a new Christian will welcome anyone who has a Bible into his home.

We must realize that those of us who minister in the Word are locked in a struggle with Satan for the souls of men. Satan doesn't attack with knives and guns. He uses smooth talking men in pin-striped suits and he can make his message sound quite authentic to those who are only partially informed. Paul placed high priority on equipping the saints "so that we may no longer be children tossed about with every wind of doctrine by the cunning of men and by their craftiness in deceitful wiles" (Ephesians 4:14).

Em Griffin suggests that a part of the training of a new Christian should include what he calls the "inoculation theory." He believes that it's possible to develop a vaccine for heresy. Most of us have taken smallpox vaccinations. As small amounts of the smallpox toxin were scratched into our skin, a sore developed, accompanied by itchiness and inflammation. The purpose of the vaccine is to produce an immunity to the disease.

Griffin describes how this technique was given a spiritual application in a camp designed to assist young people who were preparing to enter secular colleges:

> Perhaps the most effective technique the camp employed was having counselors play different types of people the students would meet the following year. One counselor wore a sign that said, "athe-

ist," for the entire week. He would talk with individual campers at meals and around the grounds trying to get them to adopt this point of view. If the student had difficulty defending the Christian position, the counselor would step out of his role and help him see the inconsistent assumptions of the atheistic position. Other staff acted different roles—scientific determinist, Communist, Playboy, Humanist, Skeptic, Buddhist, and Mormon. In this way, the students were aware of opposing points of view and had practice in dealing with them without going in over their heads. They became well prepared to be the Christian salt of the campus without losing their savour.[9]

Techniques will vary with the situation. Informational needs will depend on the nature of the Satanic attack, but every Christian needs access to resources which will help him in the struggle for his mind.

5. *Other areas of information.* Many other areas of information will need to be given to the new Christian. Above all, he needs some good tools to become an independent Bible student. He will need help in selecting a usable study Bible. Several excellent ones are on the market. The *Thompson Chain Reference Bible,* a time-honored study tool, has recently been published with a New International Version text. The *Harper Study Bible* is based on a Revised Standard Version text. I mention these two because they are based on texts which are more readable for the new Christian than those based on the older versions. Guidance should also be given to the new Christian in selecting such study aids as concordances, Bible dictionaries, and atlases. Some people mistakenly rush out to purchase the most inexpensive study helps, and they usually get what they pay for.

In chapter 3, we talked about the importance of understanding the undenominational nature of the church. This seems to be one of the most difficult subjects for new Christians to grasp. The American religious scene is so thoroughly denominational in its makeup that it's hard for people to see how undenominational Christianity is even possible. Some of the clearest thinking that's been done in recent times on this subject has been given expression in the writings of Monroe Hawley of Milwaukee, Wisconsin. His book *Searching for a Better Way* attempts to explain the undenominational concept to people who have not yet become Christians. It will also be helpful for a new Christian. An earlier book, *Redigging the Wells,* will be beneficial to the person who is attempting to facilitate the growth of a new Christian. His newest book, *The Focus of Our Faith,* defends the principle of restoring New Testament Christianity.

New Christians also need to know how to relate to the wider world. It's very difficult to suggest a complete bibliography to aid Christians in their understanding of the world of politics, sociology, psychology, and the broad range of human problems. We must not allow the Christian to think that all his concerns are wrapped up inside the walls of the church building. He must understand how God wants him to behave in the family setting, in the local community, and in the larger world community. Rubel Shelly has written an excellent book which contributes to this part of a Christian's growth, entitled *Going On to Maturity.*

There's a growing awareness of our need to develop a social conscience. Because we've seen churches abandon the saving gospel to concentrate their energies on a social gospel, we've just about left most of our social concern up to other people. Actually, restoration churches have a mixed record on social issues. We've avoided some issues altogether—world hunger, joblessness, human rights, environmental concerns, world peace, and racial discrimination. On the other hand, we've plunged headlong into some other issues without seemingly bothering to check whether our direction is in line with the Scriptures. Such issues include television, abortion, gay rights, pari-mutuel gambling, and liquor by the drink.

A few books have been written by Bible-believing people who are concerned about the Christian social conscience.

131

Among these are *Obscenity, Pornography and Censorship* by Perry C. Cotham; *Involvement: Being a Responsible Christian in a Non-Christian Society* by John R. W. Stott; and the *Christian Manifesto* by Francis Schaeffer. These books don't all speak with one voice on social issues. With respect to social issues, Bible believers scatter themselves along a pendulum which starts with Jerry Falwell on the right and ends up with Senator Mark Hatfield of Oregon on the left. All these people do agree on one thing: that the church needs to be equipping its people to have the kind of integrity that's needed to leave the church building and go into the arena of community issues and make their voices heard. It seems criminal to leave all the debate in the hands of those who have little or no respect for God. As Stott sees it,

> Some Christians, anxious above all to be faithful to the revelation of God without compromise, ignore the challenges of the modern world and live in the past. Others, anxious to respond to the world around them, trim and twist God revelation in their search for relevance. I have struggled to avoid both traps. The Christian is at liberty to surrender neither to antiquity nor modernity.[10]

Conclusion

In attempting to meet the information needs of a new Christian, the emphasis needs to be long on providing study skills and short on prepackaged answers. There may be times when a new Christian will need to be given "cook book" answers, especially when his faith is attacked by sharp antagonists, but in the main our goal should be that of developing independent thinkers who have the tools to dig information out of God's Word for themselves.

There's a risk in serving as a facilitator. The persons we try to help may not always agree with our conclusions. That's a crushing blow to egocentric mentors who want to control others, but most of us will be able to survive the experience of having a student disagree with some of our cherished positions. In the long run, the church will be blessed with healthier and more stable Christians if we produce thinkers rather than robots who feed back information that's been programmed into their minds.

Questions for Discussion

1. What is the difference between indoctrination and education?
2. What principles should a discipler observe in order to avoid becoming a manipulator?
3. Why is the "expert" not the ideal person to transmit information to the new Christian?
4. How can we reinforce the genuineness of a new Christian's conversion?
5. Why is it necessary to do this?
6. List some areas of temptation which the new Christian is likely to face.
7. How can we help with the "culture shock" that an unchurched person experiences when he comes into the body of Christ?
8. What resources would you offer in helping a new Christian learn to pray?
9. What should you do when a new Christian tells you he thinks he's committed the "unpardonable sin"?
10. What additional informational needs does a new Christian have besides the ones discussed in this chapter?

Endnotes

[1]Flavil R. Yeakley, Jr., *Why Churches Grow*, 3rd. ed. (Broken Arrow, Oklahoma: Christian Communications, Inc., 1979), p. 57.

[2]The author is planning a joint writing project with Jim Holston to produce a new Christian's study guide which will include many of the informational needs discussed in this chapter.

[3]Yeakley, *Why Churches Grow*, p. 12.

[4]*Ibid.*, pp. 11-12.

[5]Joseph C. Aldrich, *Lifestyle Evangelism* Portland, Oregon: Multnomah Press, 1981), p. 19.

[6]*Ibid.*, p. 20.

[7]Charles Mylander, *Secrets for Growing Churches* (San Francisco: Harper and Row, 1979), p. 43.

[8]For information on understanding the mindset of unchurched people consult J. Russell Hale, *The Unchurched—Who Are They and Why Do They Stay Away?* (San Francisco: Harper and Row, 1980).

[9]Em Griffin, *The Mindchangers* (Wheaton, Illinois: Tyndale House Publishers, Inc., 1976), p. 177.

[10]John R. W. Stott, *Involvement: Being a Responsible Christian in a Non-Christian Society* (Old Tappan, New Jersey: Fleming H. Revell Company, 1984), p. 14.

Chapter Ten

How Does a New Christian Find His Place in the Church?

Chapter one included a sampling of conclusions reached by different authors who have expressed their views about how actual church growth ought to be counted. They unanimously agreed that we should count only those people who become productive members. This means that church leaders need to place a high priority on helping new members become functionally active. Consequently, "new believers as soon as possible should be integrated into the life of the local church."[1]

The testimony of scripture clearly indicates that first-century Christians became functionally active in a very short period following their conversion. On the heels of the dynamic harvest of souls on the day of Pentecost, Luke says, "And they devoted themselves to the apostles' teaching and fellowship, to the breaking of bread and prayers" (Acts 2:42). That was followed by benevolent activities, attendance at the temple, daily sharing of food, and the enrichment of their devotional lives, along with evangelistic sharing of the word (Acts 2:43-47).

By the time a food crisis arose among the Hellenistic widows, some Christians in that fellowship had matured to the point that they were recognized as "men of good repute, full of the spirit and of wisdom" (Acts 6:3). Their progress had been so remarkable that they were put in charge of food distribution, and the whole church was pleased with the way the problem was handled.

The first missionary trip undertaken by Paul and Barnabas shows additional significant evidence of rapid functional growth in the early church. In their travels through Asia Minor, they covered some of the same ground twice. In their first swing through, they shared the gospel and made converts (Acts 13:43, 48; 14:1, 20). After they were thrown out of Lystra, the two preachers went on to Derbe and then doubled back on a trip through Lystra, Iconium, and Antioch of Pisidia. Their purpose on the second trip was the strengthening of the disciples. Acts 14:23 indicates how rapidly the functional growth of the disciples took place: "And when they had appointed elders for them in every church with prayer and fasting, they committed them to the Lord in whom they had believed." Every indication points to the conclusion that the functional growth of the new Christians in New Testament times took place fairly rapidly.

Gene Getz has correctly observed, "A functioning body or "body life' as some have designated it is absolutely essential for growth and maturity to take place in the church."[2] It is imperative for new members to be encouraged to participate in that body life to the level of their ability as soon as possible. A new member of the body who is not given a function falls victim to the law of disuse and becomes a liability rather than an asset.

How the New Christian Develops Functionally

1. *He learns to discover his gifts.* The Scriptures frequently speak of gifts which are employed in the church for a variety of reasons. Quite often when the subject of spiritual gifts comes up for discussion, people automatically think about supernatural gifts. Miraculous gifts in the early church were

given to supply foundational support to the church as it passed through its infant stages. The Scriptures clearly indicate that a cessation of these gifts is anticipated (1 Corinthians 13:8). The gifts appear to have been transmitted through the laying on of the apostles' hands (Acts 8:18). Since there are no living apostles alive to transmit the gifts, we may safely conclude that they have ceased as anticipated.

This does not, however, mean that the church is without gifts. In 1 Peter 4:10, the exiles of the Dispersion were told, "As each one has received a gift, employ it for one another, as good stewards of God's varied grace." Peter's thought indicates that every child of God possesses at least one gift.

So what are these gifts? Paul mentions seven of them in Romans 12:6-8: "Having gifts that differ according to the grace given to us, let us use them; if prophecy in proportion to our faith, if service in our serving; he who teaches, in his teaching, he who exhorts in his exhortation, he who contributes in liberality, he who gives aid with zeal, he who does acts of mercy with cheerfulness." The only one of these gifts that we might question in the church today is the gift of prophecy. If we think the matter through, we'll realize that prophecy need not be thought of in terms of inspired prophecy. Prophecy doesn't always involve predicting the future. The major work of the prophets was that of proclaiming the relevance of God's message to the people. Surely that gift is still needed, and that part of it, at least, remains intact.

We shouldn't limit our perception of gifts to those seven traits listed in Romans 12. There are probably many more gifts from God available for use in his service today. Some brothers have building and grounds maintenance gifts, and these are no less gifts from God. A good brother with ingenious hands used to find magnificent things to do with his wood lathe. He was always creating functional and decorative additions to our facilities. I stood back in amazement at the things he created out of his imagination, and sometimes I felt a little bit inferior when I compared his woodworking skills to my own. But if I said anything about it, he would laugh and say, "Don't worry about it, preacher, I can't preach."

We must not, however, assume that gifts and talents are the same thing. A gift is an enablement from God to make it possible for us to offer service in his Kingdom. Gifts may overlap with talents or they may not. In one congregation, a certain brother was employed as a mechanic in the secular world. To our surprise, he absolutely refused to work on buses, vans, and other church-owned vehicles. When he was asked to explain his refusal, he said, "I enjoy my work, but forty hours a week is enough of it. I'd rather do something different for the Lord." As it turned out, his refusal ended up being a stroke of genius. He became fascinated with the mechanics of the Bible school program and became a competent chairman of the educational committee. Working on vehicles would have been a tremendous waste of his gifts.

How does one discover his gifts? C. Peter Wagner suggests five tests.[3]

(1) "Explore the possibilities." A person needs to know what God wants done in ministry. We can determine that by studying the Scriptures to see how God has arranged his program for making sons and daughters out of the men and women who populate the earth. There are also some practical tests tied in with our culture and our times which should be included. The Bible doesn't speak of a building and grounds ministry, but our contemporary situation makes the need obvious.

(2) "Experiment with as many as possible." Many people have concluded that they don't have certain gifts, but they've never really tried to function in those areas, either. Quite often, church members assume they don't possess the evangelistic gift, even though they've never tried to share the gospel with even one lost person. Many people have discovered their evangelistic gift simply by trying it. To their great surprise, they were good at it. One should never eliminate a certain gift from his list until he has experimented.

(3) "Examine your feelings." A person should either en-

joy or receive a sense of satisfaction out of what he's doing for the Lord. If every moment spent in a certain type of ministry is a moment of misery, either one is functioning outside his gift area or he needs an overhaul on his attitude.

(4) "Evaluate your effectiveness." Specific, recognizable objectives should be achieved as a result of the effort given to various tasks and roles.

(5) "Expect confirmation from the body." Often we are blind to both our successes and our failures. Others can help us to be more objective in determining whether our ministry involvement is contributing to body life.

Jim Woodell has given a considerable amount of thought to the subject of finding one's gift. His thoughts are published in a work called *Equipping the Saints for the Work of Service.* He includes a gifts test to help Christians discover their gifts. Woodell notes:

> Knowing what my gift is will make it possible for me to better use my time. I will know when to say "no" to a request to do something that is not compatible with my abilities. It may be that we have assumed responsibilities which God did not intend us to have or we may have assumed responsibilities which actually detract from our basic motivation. I need to give priority in my schedule to those things that I am best suited in doing.[4]

2. *He learns to commit his resources.* It is interesting to observe that the passage on gifts in Romans 12 is preceded by an appeal to give ourselves in sacrificial service to the Lord: "I appeal to you, therefore, brethren by the mercies of God, to present your bodies as a living sacrifice, holy and acceptable to God which is your spiritual worship" (Romans 12:1). Thus we are to give no less than ourselves into the great cause of Christ. The new Christian must be taught that his relationship with Christ is more than a small compartment of interest.

Some Christians like to practice what I call *Time* magazine Christianity. *Time* is divided into departments—the world, the nation, business, sports, entertainment, the arts, books, and sometimes there's even room for a page or so about religion. Many people attempt to conduct their lives the very same way. They divide it up into work, family, school, recreation, and there's a little niche of time carved out for Christ and the church. Although the *Time* magazine version of Christianity prevails in the lives of many who claim to be Christians, the Word of God makes it clear that our love for Christ ought to consume us entirely.

Unfortunately, some disciplers attempt to develop commitment by laying guilt trips on those who seem to be deficient in their commitment. While it's to be admitted that godly sorrow has to precede repentance (2 Corinthians 7:10), the Bible's strongest motivation is the love of Christ. Paul says very simply, "For the love of Christ controls us, because we are convinced that one has died for all, though we all have died" (2 Corinthians 5:14). Could it be that godly sorrow is produced more by the realization that we have cheated ourselves in failing to appreciate the magnitude of the love of Christ, than by convincing us that we're going to Hell if we don't become more active in the church?

As a preacher of the gospel, I spent many years scolding Christians in an effort to spur them on to more energetic service. Sometimes it worked for a while. Sensitive souls would rush to the front of the auditorium during the invitation with tears streaming down their faces as they announced their desire to rededicate themselves in God's service. Some grew discouraged when their lives didn't change much after that, and they quit altogether. Very little was accomplished in terms of long-term commitment of resources to Christ. No one was rejoicing, and yet, as I understand the scriptural call to action, joy should indeed follow service. There's something wrong in a church where there's never an occasion for celebration.

3. *The new Christian needs to receive recognition for his achievements.* The American public is achievement-oriented. Track coaches measure achievement through precisely calibrated

stopwatches. Supervisors in factories gauge achievement by production output. Marketing people pay close attention to sales records.

The church isn't like the world of business and sports, but people in the church do have the need to be praised, to be congratulated and given positive strokes for giving themselves to God's service.

According to one prevailing theory, however, ministry is nothing more than a matter of duty, and why should anyone be praised for his ministry? He's just doing his duty. I've been a preacher for thirty years, and I don't preach to hear people sing my praises, but I think I'd become very discouraged if I had to go even one year without hearing someone compliment my pulpit efforts. I'd have serious doubts about the quality of my performance. I might even start questioning my gift. How can we expect Christians to function faithfully in other roles if no one ever notices? Unfortunately, there are some tasks—like preparing communion, opening and closing the building, and keeping the ice and snow scraped off the sidewalks—that we never seem to notice until the person who has been doing it decides to quit. As the old saying goes, "We never miss the water until the well runs dry."

Achievement is admittedly harder to measure in the spiritual realm than it is in some other areas. After all, you can't put a stopwatch on love, joy, peace, patience, kindness, goodness, faithfulness, gentleness, and self-control There's no way to graph sincerity out on a chart, but the keen-eyed Christian can observe indications of growth—a brother reads the Bible through in a year; another gets up an hour before work time to study every morning; someone else starts visiting shut-ins. When these things are noticed and appreciation is expressed, the person doing those things may say, "Oh, it's nothing," but you can be sure that person will be encouraged to continue.

Even though there seems to be a certain reticence about affirming people in their progress, we are on very safe scriptural grounds to do so. Paul tells the Romans, "Love one another with brotherly affection; outdo one another in showing honor" (Romans 12:10). In 1 Timothy 5:17, the apostle says, "Let the elders who rule well be counted worthy of double honor, especially those who labor in preaching and teaching." Nearly every New Testament epistle begins with words of commendation and encouragement. To love one another is to affirm one another, praise one another, and rejoice with one another. We need more celebration in the church.

We need to be more creative in learning how to do this. I've known some thoughtful Christians who planned a birthday party on the anniversary of a new Christian's baptism. Others send cards, flowers, and small gifts to recognize and celebrate spiritual achievements. The congregation where I preach has given me three appreciation dinners and a congregational picnic in my honor during the ten years I've been with them. That probably helps explain why my tenure has been twice as long with this church as it has been with any other. But it's not just the preacher who needs that kind of shot in the arm, it's everyone—the church secretary, the custodian, the elders. . . . I know one brother who buys tickets to very expensive entertainment events and asks people to go with him if they have shown unusual dedication. At a recent Vacation Bible School closing program, I gave out a special "preacher's award" to those who had worked above and beyond the call of duty. There are many ways to celebrate achievement. We are limited only by the size of our imaginations. However we do it, we must convey the message to new Christians that what they do has value.

Questions for Discussion

1. What dynamic enabled the new members of the church in Jerusalem and the churches in Asia Minor to experience such rapid functional growth?
2. Which of these factors are relevant to our contemporary culture?
3. What does the term "body life" mean?
4. Why is it important for a new Christian to discover his gifts?
5. Does everyone have the gift of evangelism?
6. What additional suggestions would you offer to help a new Christian discover his gifts?
7. What is the most effective way to encourage a new Christian to commit his resources to God?
8. Why does guilt motivation frequently fail to produce the desired results?
9. Why do new Christians need to be recognized for their achievements?
10. How can we help new Christians celebrate their progress?

Endnotes

[1]Gene Getz, *Sharpening the Focus of the Church* (Chicago, Illinois: Moody Press, 1974), p. 47.

[2]*Ibid.*, p. 116.

[3]C. Peter Wagner, *Your Church Can Grow* (Glendale, California: Regal Books, 1976), p. 74.

[4]Jim Woodell, *Equipping the Saints for the Work of Serving* (Privately Published, 1977), p. 4.

Chapter Eleven

The Emotional Needs of the New Christian

If a new Christian is to develop Christlike behavior, he must grow emotionally. In our brotherhood, there is a healthy suspicion of emotionalism. We have observed other religious systems which are governed almost entirely by emotional reactions, and we have concluded that zeal without knowledge is a dangerous thing. It's possible, however, to overreact to the dangers of emotionalism. Sometimes we forget that everyone has feelings. When we respond to the Lord, we respond with the total person, and that includes our emotions.

Lon Woodrum has suggested, "A person without emotion would be an animated clod or a monster. Emotion is as much a part of man as his nervous system."[1] Feelings may be an unreliable barometer of one's spiritual condition, but no person who truly turns his life over to God does so without feeling. Along with encouraging the new Christian to approach his discipleship logically, we need also to remember that a part of discipleship involves being "aglow with the Spirit" (Romans 12:11).

Biblical Teaching Concerning Emotions

The ancient men of God were not unfeeling scholars who pronounced dry propositional statements without emotion. David writes, "I am weary from my moaning; every night I flood my bed with tears; I drench my couch with weeping" (Psalm 6:6). Elijah's emotions plunged to rock bottom when he sat beneath a broom tree and "asked that he might die' (1 Kings 19:4). Jeremiah is remembered as "the weeping prophet" largely because he let loose a flood tide of emotions in Lamentations as he surveyed the carnage in his beloved Jerusalem. He writes, "Is it nothing to you, all you who pass by? Look and see if there is any sorrow like my sorrow which was brought upon me, which the Lord inflicted on the day of his fierce anger" (Lamentations 1:12).

New Testament personalities ran the range of highs and lows in their emotional responses. Peter was literally ecstatic when he stood with the Lord on the Mount of Transfiguration and proposed the erection of three tabernacles, one to the honor of Moses, one to the honor of Elijah, and one to the honor of the Lord (Matthew 17:4). On the other hand, no one ever felt more depressed than Peter when he denied Jesus. Mark tells us that "he broke down and wept" (Mark 14:72). Surely it's appropriate for the Christians who have already weathered some of life's storms to help those new members of the body in their emotional growth.

Emotional Needs of New Christians

The new Christian comes into the faith with a variety of emotional needs. We can probably expect most new Christians to be somewhat maladjusted when they start their walk with the Lord. I'm not suggesting that all new Christians are candidates for the psychiatric ward. I'm not even saying they need professional counseling. But the fact remains that people don't usually seek new patterns of living if they are completely satisfied with the old ones. The

146

discipling process requires mature Christians to involve themselves in bringing the new Christians to maturity.

1. *New Christians need to find constructive outlets for their enthusiasm.* When sinners are brought to Christ and come to a realization of the implications of forgiveness, it quite naturally excites them. They are anxious to share this new dimension of their lives. Quite often such persons crave involvement in the works of ministry. Unfortunately, this surge of enthusiasm often collides with a wall of inertia when new Christians verbalize their enthusiasm to apathetic church members. Bored brethren can quickly extinguish the fires of enthusiasm with their placid attitudes and cynical remarks. In too many cases, new Christians have either joined the army of apathetic adherents or withdrawn from involvement altogether.

2. *New Christians need warmth.* The new Christian must know that his fellow Christians see him as a valued and treasured member of the Lord's body. He must not become just another statistic. He needs acceptance and affirmation.

The reader is referred to the discussion in chapter 8 for practical suggestions on how warmth can be communicated. Caring needs to be verbalized as well as shown. The church at Philippi certainly must have felt the warmth in their relationship to Paul when he wrote, "I hold you in my heart, for you are all partakers with me of grace" (Philippians 1:7).

A few years ago I met a man who helped me a great deal. On the surface he was a little bit irritating. He was the kind of person who challenged some of my long-cherished beliefs. He forced me to think through some of my beliefs which I had always taken for granted. I came out a stronger person because of my relationship with him. One day he was tragically killed in a freak accident. I have always regretted that I never once told him that I appreciated his contributions to my life. For some reason, we seem always to be holding back words of love. Perhaps it's because we're turned off by those who overdo it, but we really need to let people know how much we cherish their friendship.

It is sad when two people come together and like what they see in each other, but they never verbalize their feelings. A relationship that might have been, crashed before it even has a chance to get off the ground. The tragedy is that love goes unrequited simply because it is undeclared.[2]

3. *New Christians need to be encouraged to develop emotional independence.* There comes a time when we must give the new Christian some space. Sometimes it's possible to be so concerned about the spiritual development of a new member of the body that we smother him with too much attention. In the final analysis, the more mature Christian actually does nothing more than facilitate growth. He can encourage, assist, comfort, correct, admonish, rebuke, praise, and love, but he cannot grow for the other person. The new Christian must desire to grow from within. He must actually want to become a productive, well-adjusted member of God's family. There is a point at which nurturing stops and responsibility begins.

How much help is too much? There's no pat answer to that question. The mature Christian who wants to serve as an enabler must develop sensitivity to the emotional needs of his new brother or sister. He must be able to read the verbal and nonverbal signals which say, "You're crowding too close. Would you please back off and let me breathe a little?" Great wisdom and fervent prayer are required to know when that point has been reached.

Helping the New Christian Find Joy

It's probably not realistic to expect a perpetual state of happiness to suddenly invade a person's life when he becomes a Christian. The term "happy" is rooted in the Old English word "happenstance," which implied pleasant circumstances. Christian joy runs considerably deeper than that. Paul was able to assert his joy from a prison cell when he wrote to the Philippians, "I shall rejoice" (Philippians 1:19).

Later he said, "I have learned in whatever state I am to be content" (Philippians 4:11).

Part of the assimilation process involves helping Christians learn Paul's secret of maintaining an upbeat attitude. His positive viewpoint surfaced in the dampness of his prison cell because he had developed the spiritual and emotional maturity which undergird a person in times of trouble and danger. He said, "I know how to be abased and I know how to abound in any and all circumstances. I have learned the secret of facing plenty and hunger, abundance and want" (Philippians 4:12-13). Paul's secret was not some kind of special gift that God makes available to those with an apostolic calling. It's a universal blessing which God offers the entire Christian community. In 2 Timothy 1:7, Paul suggests that "God did not give us a spirit of timidity, but a spirit of power and love and self control." The King James Version translates "self control" as "a sound mind." This suggests that sound minds are normative among people who walk with Jesus.

As new Christians come into our fellowship, we have an opportunity to help them claim these valuable gifts. Furthermore, it's quite likely that our new brother or sister will be seeking some assistance in building a more joyous life. "There seems to be a definite correlation between an individual's motivational needs stage and that of the person or group which is most likely to lead him to conversion."[3]

Students of psychology have long recognized that all human beings possess certain needs which must be fulfilled if they are to live useful and productive lives. These needs are cyclical in nature, which is to say that they recur with regularity. For example, if you eat a meal at noontime, your need for food will then be satisfied, but the need will recur again by suppertime on the same day. Our needs begin with basic physical things and then progress upward to such things as emotional fulfillment. Dr. Bob Rigdon of Western Carolina University has adapted A. H. Maslow's famous hierarchy of needs in the following form.

Adult Human Needs

(Hierarchical Order of Prepotency)

1. Physical—Food, Air, Water, Sex (eros), Activity, Elimination, Sleep, etc.
2. Safety, Security
3. Play, Laughter, Humor
4. Love, Belongingness, Nonsexual
   A. Agape B. Philia C. Storge D. Need to father or bear a child.
5. Self-Respect, Esteem, Worth
6. Information
7. Understanding, Wisdom
8. Self-Actualization
   A. Why am I here?
   B. Where did I come from?
   C. Where am I going?[4]

Dr. Rigdon notes, "Each category is referred to in principle in the scriptures."[5]

Part of our approach to the assimilation of new Christians will involve helping our new brothers and sisters find lawful and scriptural ways of satisfying each one of these needs. There is no need that human beings have which can't be fulfilled in a way that harmonizes with the demands of scripture. As enablers, we are challenged to direct new Christians toward finding scriptural means of meeting these needs.

1. *We must be able to recognize the potential in people.* How many people would have seen Peter and Andrew as future apostles while they worked at their fishing trade on the Sea of Galilee? When Jesus said to them, "Follow me and I will make you fishers of men" (Matthew 4:19), he looked beyond their coarseness, their lack of education, and their worldly ways. He saw gospel preachers!

The new Christian who comes to us may look like nothing but trouble on the surface. He may be so loaded down with insecurities, anxieties, and immoral excesses that we feel totally inadequate as enablers. If, on the other hand, we'll simply recognize that he's made in God's image and that Christ died for him on Calvary, we'll begin to think in terms of what he's capable of becoming. Goethe once said, "If I treat you as you are, you will remain as you are, but if I treat you as if you were what you could become, that is what you will become."[6]

Of course, there's the possibility that you will invest time in someone's life and that person won't respond to the loving, the affirming, and the caring, but it's still worth the effort for the sake of those who do. Nobody bats 1,000 in the big leagues and nobody bats 1,000 in the big-league business of helping people grow in grace and knowledge.

2. *We must learn the principle of acceptance without approval.* Jesus acted on this principle constantly during his earthly ministry. Consider the time he and the disciples were crossing the Sea of Galilee in a boat when a sudden storm turned the placid lake into a death chamber of wind and water. The disciples were panic stricken, but Jesus was taking a nap in the stern of that little craft. The disciples clamored for his attention. They said, "Teacher, do you not care if we perish?" Their response clearly irritated Jesus. He asked, "Why are you afraid? Have you no faith?" Surely, by this time, they should have realized that Jesus possessed supernatural powers. Their low level of faith disappointed him, but he went ahead and removed their fears by calming the storm anyway (Mark 4:35-41). That's acceptance without approval.

To help a new Christian move from point A to point B, we must accept the fact that he's at point A right now. Chiding and scolding him for being at point A won't help him make progress. Withdrawing from him because you don't approve of point A will only frustrate him. We have to remember that substantial growth takes place slowly. Sometimes it's barely visible, but most progress comes about at a snail's pace. Ray Stedman's thoughts on this subject need to be heeded by Christians at all levels of maturity:

We may come into a relative degree of maturity within a few years of our conversion, but we shall be engaged in the process of growth as long as we are in this present life. After all as someone has pointed out, it takes God years to grow an oak tree, but he can grow a squash in three months. The world has seen enough of Christian squashes.[7]

3. *We need to become invisible helpers.* We need to restudy the implications of what Jesus had in mind when he said, "Beware of practicing your piety before men in order to be seen of them" (Matthew 6:1). If we become too obvious in our attempt to help, there is some reason to question whether we're giving the help to enable a new Christian to grow or meeting some of our own unfulfilled needs for recognition. Someone has said, "You can do all kinds of good if you don't care who gets the credit for it."

We also have to watch playing the rescue game. If we always make ourselves available to bail a new Christian out of trouble every time he faces a crisis, we can easily cripple him emotionally to the point that he'll never be able to stand under his own power. Besides that, the rescue game is a pretty heavy load to carry around all the time. I can't think of anything that would be more draining than to use all my energy trying to direct the spiritual and emotional program for someone else's life. In the first place, it's too tall an order. Most of us don't have enough resources on our own to meet every need another Christian has. Besides that, we run the risk of being resented when we offer help that's neither needed nor wanted.

Bruce Larson warns of the pitfall of making your help too obvious:

Down through my adolescence, adult years, and now into middle age, the people who have helped me most dramatically are people who were, I feel sure, not conscious of trying to help me. They were with me as friends, not as superior beings. But the people who have been trying more obviously to rescue me from my stupidity, ignorance, stubbornness, meanness, or blindness have probably received more resentment than gratitude.[8]

Conclusion

Part of the assimilation process in the life of the new Christian involves helping him enjoy the full and abundant life (John 10:10). Healthy emotional growth depends on one's ability to fulfill his legitimate needs within the boundaries of God's sacred teaching. Some will grow more rapidly than others. Some will make rapid progress for a while and then fall back a notch or two. Our job as enablers is to believe in the new Christian's potential, to offer help when it's needed, and to give him space when helping would really be a hindrance. Our goal is to see him become a fully self-actualized person.

Questions for Discussion

1. Define emotions.
2. What should we do when we see other Christians throwing cold water on the enthusiasm of new Christians?
3. How can we encourage new Christians to accept responsibility for their own behavior and attitudes?
4. What is the difference between happiness and joy?
5. Which of the adult human needs are likely to be more pressing in the life of someone who has been recently converted?
6. How can we develop the vision to look beyond the problems we see in the new Christian's present life to the potential he has and what he will be like when he is more nearly self-actualized?
7. What is a self-actualized person?
8. How do we demonstrate acceptance without approval?
9. Why is it important to become invisible helpers?
10. What are some of the pitfalls of the rescue game?

Endnotes

[1]Lon Woodrum, *Christianity Today*, January 7, 1966.

[2]Alan Loy McGinnis, *The Friendship Factor* (Minneapolis, Minnesota: Augsburg Publishing House, 1979), p. 44.

[3]Keith Miller, *The Becomers* (Waco, Texas: Word Books, 1977), p. 78.

[4]Bob Rigdon, *Happiness Explained* (Sylva, North Carolina: Privately published by the author, Bob Rigdon; P. O. Box 985, Sylva, North Carolina 28779, 1983), p. 38.

[5]*Ibid.*

[6]Quoted by Dave Grant, *The Ultimate Power* (Old Tappan, New Jersey: Fleming H. Revell, Co., 1983), p. 46.

[7]Ray C. Stedman, *Body Life* 2nd ed. (Glendale, California: Regal Book Division, G/L Publications, 1977), p. 136.

[8]Keith Miller and Bruce Larson, *The Passionate People* (Waco, Texas: Word Books, 1980), p. 32.

Chapter Twelve

Goals for the Christian

The new Christian assumes the responsibility of functioning as salt, light and leaven in the world. We assist him in taking on these traits by encouraging him to establish some tangible goals. Jesus honored goal setting when he said, "For which of you desiring to build a tower, does not first sit down and count the cost, whether he has enough to complete it. Otherwise when he has laid a foundation, and is not able to finish, all who see it will mock him" (Luke 14:28-29). In this statement Jesus provided two insights into goal setting: (1) He gave his endorsement to the practice of advance planning, and (2) he suggested the wisdom of realistically evaluating the chances of success before embarking on some kind of project.

In helping new Christians establish goals, the following principles should be observed.[1]

1. *Goals should be consistent with scripture.* Second Timothy 3:16-17 offers us an explanation of the purpose of the Bible: "All scripture is inspired by God and profitable for teaching, for reproof, for correction, and for training in righteousness, that the man of God may be complete, equipped for every good work." This means that the new Christian needs constant exposure to the Word as he plans objectives

and involves himself actively in attempting to reach those objectives.

In chapter 9, some suggestions were offered concerning a study Bible and additional study resources. The new Christian needs a plan for using those resources. He needs to make time in his schedule for Bible reading and Bible study. Bible reading and Bible study aren't the same thing. In Bible reading, a person simply sits down and reads through a portion of the text and meditates on it. In Bible study a person wrestles with things like word meanings, the historical context, and application. We all need time to do both. One way to read the Bible profitably is to set a goal for reading the Bible through. Several different programs have been devised to enable a person to go through the Bible in a year. A study plan would probably involve a specific book or a specific Biblical topic.

Another helpful approach to regular Bible reading calls for the use of some of the devotional guides which are available on the commercial market. Twentieth Century Christian publishes an excellent devotional guide which includes a suggested scripture reading for each day and a brief essay written about the suggested reading. The publication is called *Power For Today*.[2]

However a new Christian may choose to structure his Bible reading and Bible study program, he must make room in his life to let God speak to him through the Word. His goals ought to include a plan for allowing that process to take place.

2. *Goals should enrich relationships.* It is possible to know the Bible from Genesis to maps and become so thoroughly grounded in the truth as to be able to prevail in debate with any false teacher and yet strike out as a person. The Scriptures remind us that "none of us lives to himself, and none of us dies to himself" (Romans 14:7). In that same general context, the author says, "We who are strong ought to bear with the failings of the weak and not to please ourselves; let each of us please his neighbor for his own good, to edify him" (Romans 15:1-2). We haven't been brought into the

body merely to save our own souls and to build our own little islands of peace and safety. We are here to encourage one another, and we must help new Christians reach out to others with acts of caring.

3. *Goals should be selected which can be mutually owned by other Christians.* It's interesting to note that Ephesians 4 is a chapter about building up the body, but it starts with an appeal for unity. Paul begs his readers to be "eager to maintain the unity of the Spirit in the bond of peace" (Ephesians 4:3). The late Ira North was so impressed with this principle that he called it "the golden key to church growth." He contended, "The number one problem in the local congregation today is keeping the unity of the Spirit in the bond of peace."[3]

In terms of goal setting for the new Christian, unity is not merely the absence of conflict; it represents a mutual determination among Christians to work together as they pursue worthwhile objectives. New brothers and sisters in Christ must be able to see that "lone ranger" Christians are not in God's plan.

4. *Goals should be selected that will survive crisis and failure.* The apostle Paul maintained enduring goals. In 2 Corinthians 4:8-9, he wrote, "We are afflicted in every way but not crushed; perplexed but not forsaken, struck down, but not destroyed." As a new Christian contemplates his goals, he should be confronted with some hard questions. What goals do you have left if you lose your job? What goals remain if you lose your spouse? What goals can you pursue if you lose your health? What goals can you claim if you go broke? The Christian who has been realistic about goal setting will never say, "I've lost everything I've ever worked for." If he feels that way, he hitched his wagon to a wrong star.

5. *New Christians need goals that will serve them through the course of an entire lifetime.* Recently my wife and I received a letter from some friends who aren't Christians. After sharing the most recent events in their lives, they related a goal statement for their future. It went something like this: "We

want to get the house paid for, get the kids educated and settled into marriages and then maybe we'll have time to travel around and see some of the country before we die." There's nothing wrong with wanting to pay off a mortgage, educate children, see them settled in happy marriages, and then taking off for the Grand Canyon, but what does a person do when he's done all that? What goals does a person still have when he's seen the Taj Mahal half a dozen times? Some people grow quite disillusioned when the fun's all done. Could that be what happened to Ernest Hemingway? to Freddie Prinze? to John Belushi? to Howard Hughes? to Janis Joplin? to Elvis Presley? and to numerous others who stood in the spotlight for a while and found it couldn't last? The new Christian must realize that he still has some worthwhile goals when the children are gone from home, when the day of retirement rolls around, and even when cancer turns every day into an experience of pain and the suffering can only temporarily be relieved by merciful shots of morphine.

The experience of Paul in prison contributes to our insight. Death was imminent as he wrote to Timothy. Nevertheless, he gave instructions to Timothy as if he planned to live another ten years: "When you come, bring the cloak that I left with Carpus at Troas, also the book and above all the parchments" (2 Timothy 5:14). Knowing he was about to die, Paul made a conscious decision (1) to take care of his body, hence the request for a cloak, and (2) to take care of his mind, as evidenced by his request for the books and the parchments. He was willing to die, but he was determined to die smart. We need to help new Christians develop that kind of zest for life.

6. *New Christians need goals which will deepen their spiritual roots.* Andrew Murray says that prayer must occupy the very highest rung on the ladder of spiritual activity.

The place and the power of prayer in the Christian life is too little understood. I feel sure that as long as we view prayer simply as a means of maintaining our own Christian lives, we will not fully understand what it is supposed to be. But when we learn to regard it as the highest part of the work entrusted to us—the root and strength of all other work—we will see there is nothing we need to practice more than the art of praying.[4]

In 1 Thessalonians 5, the apostle Paul strings out a list of recommendations for people who want to be prepared when the day of the Lord comes like a thief in the night. In verse 17 he adds this link to the chain: "Pray constantly." In Ephesians 6, the person who is armed to engage Satan in combat is told to "pray at all times in the Spirit, with all prayer and supplication. To that end keep alert with all perseverance, making supplication for all the saints" (Ephesians 6:18).

For some new Christians, learning to pray seems harder than learning to high jump eight feet. Perhaps it's the fear of praying that has caused some people to settle for liturgical forms of prayer in which one simply repeats the thoughts which have been written by others. There may well be some value in reading the prayers of others, but every new Christian needs to learn how to pray spontaneously.

But how does a new Christian get started? He needs to start by understanding that God is a heavenly Father. He wants to listen to us just as those of us who are earthly fathers want to listen to our children. My oldest son lives in Germany, and one of the most exciting experiences for me is to pick up the phone and hear him say, "Hi, Dad." Paul says, "God has sent the Spirit of his Son into your hearts, crying "Abba! Father!" (Galatians 4:6). "Abba" was the Aramaic word which suggested an intimate bonding between a child and a father. It seems disrespectful to address God by saying, "Hi, Dad," but we surely ought to avoid the other extreme of trying for flowery eloquence. Most new Christians don't know how to express themselves with "church words" anyway, and they don't have to. They just need to start talking with God about how they feel.

But what do you talk to God about? Well, you can start off with expressing gratitude. I've always been impressed with small children who thank God for the knives, the forks, the napkins, the plates, the wallpaper, and the dog who's eating his Alpo on the back porch. Maybe they're more specific than they need to be, but there's no question about the fact that they understand where our blessings originate. If you start telling God about the things you appreciate, you should be able to talk with Him for quite a long while. Then there are the things that others need—your brothers and sisters in the hospital, the kids at school, Mom and Dad back on the old home place, searching people in your community who are studying the Bible with brethren who have evangelistic gifts. There are many needs of others to be prayed about. Finally, you come to your own needs—your need to grow in grace and knowledge; your need to be able to let others see Christ in you as you go about your daily tasks; your need to discipline yourself toward the tasks of study, serving, and affirming. Again the list is long. After a while a person who follows this formula—thanksgiving, intercession, and petition—will become more comfortable in talking with God.

We need to help new Christians realize that God hears and answers prayers which are crudely worded and hastily thought out. God understands our personal weaknesses, our insecurities, our times of depression, the ever present pressures of family life, debt, and loss. He has promised, "I will never fail you nor forsake you" (Hebrews 13:5). Even when we do a very poor job of expressing our needs to God, we are assured in God's Word that He responds to our petition: "Likewise the Spirit helps us in our weakness; for we do not know how to pray as we ought, but the Spirit himself intercedes for us with sighs too deep for words and he who searches the hearts of men knows what is the mind of the Spirit, because the Spirit intercedes for the saints according to the will of God" (Romans 8:26-27).

7. *Goals should have flexibility.* Everybody needs a plan B. Again, Paul sets an example in this respect. He wanted to

see Rome. Plan A called for him to go at his own pace and in his own manner. He realized the goal, but he had to settle for plan B as his means of getting there. Plan B meant that he went as a prisoner. Our goal adjustment may not have to be that drastic, but somewhere along the line, we need to have enough flexibility in our planning to allow for circumstances which cannot be predicted. Every football coach enters the contest with a game plan. One evening while working on this part of the manuscript, I turned on the radio when I stopped for supper. A college football coach was explaining his team's loss on the previous Saturday. He said, "We worked hard on returning kickoffs. When we got the ball in the end zone, we set up our blockers for what should have been a long gain. In fact, the play was forming so well that the runner might easily have gone all the way for a touchdown. Unfortunately, one man missed his block and the runner was tackled on his own five-yard line." Every coach knows that he's going to have to alter his original game plan. Most hope they don't have to alter it immediately after the opening kickoff. Life works the same way, and we need to be able to help new Christians build enough flexibility into their goal planning so that they don't come away feeling devastated the first time they experience disappointment.

8. *Goals need to be challenging but reachable.* If a person can't carry a tune, it wouldn't be wise to encourage that person to shoot for the Metropolitan Opera. Sometimes new Christians start out with visions of grandeur that aren't realistic. Take the case of the person who announces that he's planning a career in ministry even though he hasn't been out of the baptistry long enough for his hair to dry. The subject of motivation for entering full-time ministry is beyond the scope of this book, but some people enter full-time ministry with little real aptitude for the task and with motivation that's not always honorable. No one should throw cold water on the enthusiasm of a new Christian, but if you're a real friend to a new Christian, you may have to help him see that he can serve God in the shop better than he can

in the pulpit.

At the other end of the spectrum is the person who doesn't believe he has anything to offer in the Lord's service. We need to help that person develop a vision of what he can become. Sometimes there's a fine line which separates a respectable challenge and an unbearable burden. Above all, we must help the new Christian plug into God's resources. After all, we serve a God who is "able to do far more abundantly than we ask or think" (Ephesians 3:20).

Conclusion

One final admonition about goals is in order. Practically every one of these goal principles requires us to turn loose of the things that have previously given us security. Reaching for worthwhile goals requires risk. However, the risk is a calculated risk. The leap of faith is not a leap in the dark. Abraham and Sarah took a tremendous risk when they loaded up their belongings and set out for God only knew where, but it wasn't a blind risk. God did know where, and God guided them. God has promised to be with us until the close of the age (Matthew 28:20). We'll never know just how much he is with us if we keep protecting our safety. For that reason, we will have to keep urging new Christians to move out of the safe, warm nest in which they have been spiritually incubated if they are ever to "mount up with wings like eagles" (Isaiah 40:31).

Questions for Discussion

1. Can you think of additional scriptures besides Luke 14:28-29 which endorse the practice of goal setting?
2. What suggestions would you offer a new Christian as he plans a program of Bible reading and Bible study?
3. How can we encourage new Christians to become relationship builders?
4. Is Ira North right when he calls unity the "golden key to church growth"? Why is it so important?
5. How can we reach practical agreement concerning specific ministries the church needs to get behind?
6. List some goals that will endure through crises and failures.
7. How can we remain enthusiastic about our goals all our lives?
8. What suggestions can you offer about learning to pray?
9. What questions would you pose to the new Christian who says he wants to enter full-time ministry?
10. What's the difference between a leap of faith and a leap in the dark?

Endnotes

[1]I am indebted to Landon Saunders for much of the goal-setting philosophy explained in this chapter. I have adapted, modified, and expanded his ideas to fit the new Christian's situation. His original presentation is included in the tape series *Feeling Good About Yourself.*

[2]*Power For Today* may be ordered from 20th Century Christian, P. O. Box 40304, Nashville, Tennessee 37204.

[3]Ira North, *Balance—A Tried and Tested Formula for Church Growth* (Nashville, Tennessee: Gospel Advocate Company, 1983), p. 57.

[4]Andrew Murray, *With Christ in the School of Prayer* (Springdale, Pennsylvania: Whitaker House, r.p. 1981), pp. 5-6.

Chapter Thirteen

The Dropout Problem—
The Attrition Rate
Is Too Great

The television set was tuned to the station carrying a same-day replay of the Indianapolis 500. The camera turned away from the action on the track and focused on a set of graphics which reported the attrition rate. Several cars had been forced to leave the race with engine problems, transmission failures, accident damage, and several different kinds of mechanical malfunctions. By the end of the race only about half of the thirty-three cars whose engines had roared to life in response to the familiar command, "Gentlemen, start your engines," were still able to race on the track. All the others had fallen victim to the attrition rate.

Churches experience an attrition problem in nearly equal proportions. Yeakley estimates that we are losing about one half of those whom we convert, and he finds evidence that the dropout rate is on the increase.[1] The attrition rate doesn't stop with the dropout problem. Every church has members on its roll who can be described as inactive. An inactive member is defined as one who attends with some degree of regularity but then refuses to become involved in tasks and fellowship. Inactive members never show up for the Sunday night and midweek services. Their Sunday morning attendance is a hit-or-miss proposition ranging from one to three Sundays a month. Inactives don't show up in most statistical studies. Dr. John Savage of LEAD Consultants has conducted a limited study among United Methodist churches in Western New York. He found that 33 per cent of the members in those churches fall into the inactive category.[2]

Although the dropout rate isn't normally publicized and the inactive percentage hardly receives any attention at all, every church leader knows that some folks are going out the back door. According to some people, the church can maintain a healthy growth rate if more people are coming in the front door than are dropping out of the church through the back door. Such theorists advise us to concentrate on constantly winning new people so that the percentage of those staying outweighs the percentage of those leaving. While this solution may create an illusion of healthy growth, there's surely something defective about a philosophy that treats new members as if they were chewing gum to be discarded when all the sweetness is gone.

James teaches us to value the person who has strayed away from the church: "My brethren, if any one among you wanders from the truth and someone brings him back, let him know that whoever brings back a sinner from the error of his way will save a soul from death and will cover a multitude of sins" (James 5:19-20). He claims that Christ's death covers the sins of wayward brethren just as it covers the transgression of an alien sinner.

This chapter will focus on three approaches to the dropout problem: (1) the cause, (2) prevention, and (3) cure.

Cause

People generally go from active involvement to less active, to inactive, to complete withdrawal as they slide down the dropout track. Their reasons are varied and complex.

We must be careful about jumping to overly simplistic conclusions when we see people moving in the direction of inactivity. We have a tendency to be judgmental, opinionated, and resentful when we see our brethren begin to lose interest in the church. We can't help them by becoming defensive. Sometimes we'll have to admit that our approach to things has made it easy for members to become less active. That's not an easy indictment to accept, but it's essential to swallow that pill if we really want to achieve success in closing the back door.

J. Russell Hale conducted his research among the unchurched, many of whom have dropped out of previous involvement with churches. At the end of his research, he concluded,

> Unless one can hear and feel the anguish, sometimes the bitterness and hostility, of those who are alienated from churches—as indeed echoes of one's own latent frustrations and failures—one will fail in one's best efforts to proclaim the good news.[3]

An example of the kind of anguish Hale encountered is seen in the comments of a lady who left a circle of religious involvement which she describes as the "Protestant lunatic fringe, Church of Christ, Baptist varieties and Pentecostal varieties."[4] She writes:

> Most of us who left simply consigned ourselves to lives of misery on earth and eternity of hell after death. We felt God's hate for us was too great to appease, that God seemed to hate everything, even the light of the sun. In spite of all the bibliolatry these churches teach, if a person chanced on a sublime and beautiful passage such as "doubtless thou art our Father even though Abraham be ignorant of us all," or "all shall be taught from the greatest to the least," that person was immediately strongly reprimanded. Such

beauty did not enter into such a monstrous, ugly god's "plan of salvation."[5]

One is tempted to offer a rebuttal to such caustic remarks, but perhaps it's best to let it stand as a reminder of how we are sometimes viewed by the dropout. We must be able to evaluate the causes of spiritual inactivity by objective criteria before we can go to work on prevention and cure.

Psychological Causes

1. *Anxiety.* In his research project among the United Methodist churches, John Savage discovered that quite frequently an incident occurs within the church setting which "produces some kind of anxiety, making the individual feel uncomfortable."[6] When a person becomes uncomfortable in the church setting, he then proceeds toward withdrawal.

2. *Personality differences.* Quite often a disagreement with some member of the church, coupled with either inability or unwillingness to resolve the conflict, causes a person to become less active. One such member explained his absence from the church services this way: "I had a run-in with this one elder." The same kind of threatening conflict might well take place with the preacher, with a family member who is active in the church, or with any regularly attending church member.

3. *Personal stress.* Sometimes people withdraw into a cocoon when they're faced with personal problems. Some personal problems cause people to feel isolated. Shame and guilt are often associated with such stresses, which then give way to the lethargy that seems to go with depression. To such persons, church involvement means just one more stress. Some people have been led to believe that the Christian life is a problem-free existence. They think, "If I were really the kind of Christian I'm supposed to be, I wouldn't have these problems." They may also fear exposure and rebuke from the body.

4. *Burnout.* Some people quit because they don't seem to

be able to stay motivated. When Hale conducted his research among the unchurched people living in retirement communities in Florida, he interviewed many of the people who recalled having been active in churches "up north." But now they felt used up. As they saw it, they had done their part. It was time to turn over the church work to younger people who have more energy.[7]

Others who suffer from the burnout syndrome aren't in their retirement years, but they drop out because they feel exploited, they feel their interests have outgrown what the church has to offer, and they have bad memories of the religion that was "crammed down their throats" during childhood.

Theological Causes

1. *Differences in religious backgrounds.* Churches of Christ are unique in the religious community in that we stress unswerving allegiance to Biblical authority and in that our hermeneutical approach involves interpreting the Bible just as we would any other piece of literature. This puts us at odds with liberal Protestants, whose anti-supernatural bias forces them to interpret all miraculous Biblical events as mythical stories with symbolic meanings, as suggested by Bultmann and others. It also finds us at odds with most fundamentalist groups who depend on the illumination of the Holy Spirit to guide them to correct Biblical interpretation. Many of us find ourselves embarrassed to be classified with the fundamentalists when some rather vocal fundamentalists are making news headlines by claiming to have the correct Christian slant on such varied issues as prayers in schools, apartheid in South Africa, and the proliferation of the nuclear arms race. When someone comes into our fellowship from a position either far to the left or far to the right of our own theological orientation, he is more likely to leave than a person who started out nearer to what we believe. Yeakley discovered that "those whose original theological position was already similar to that of the church

of Christ are less likely to convert and more likely to drop out if they do convert."[8]

Yeakley also discovered that people don't usually remain in our fellowship unless they were dissatisfied either with their secular life styles or with their previous religious teachings prior to conversion. Of those who say they were satisfied with their previous beliefs and life styles prior to a contact from someone in the church, 90 per cent eventually drop out.[9]

2. *Worship structure.* Many new members have difficulty handling the structure of worship in the Churches of Christ. The absence of instrumental music is the most noticeable problem. The problem is minimal in those larger churches where there's a decent sprinkling of people who know how to sing on key, trained song leaders, and a balance of parts. It's a much larger problem in the smaller churches whose song leaders have never received any musical training and whose qualifications for leading consist mainly of nerve and gall. Too often the songs drag along at a snail's pace, the pitch is consistently too high or too low, and the congregation pays little attention to musical notation. In that setting, the structure of the song service can be quite discouraging for the new member, especially if the new member has musical training.

People who come into our fellowship from Catholic churches often miss the statuary, the liturgy, and the stations of the cross. Somehow it seems irreverent to approach God without genuflection. While they may be dissatisfied with Catholic viewpoints, they find it much harder to break away from lifelong conditioning with regard to the structure of worship.

3. *Threats to personal independence.* Some leave because they feel restricted by the viewpoints which the leadership expects them to adopt. The more rigid and specific a church becomes in this respect, the more dropouts it's likely to have among those who yearn for freedom. An example of such restrictions is seen in churches where the leadership insists that only the King James Version of the Bible be read in the

public services. Some people will leave rather than put up with that kind of confinement.

4. *An anti-institutional stance.* Ever since the social upheaval of the sixties, there has been a vocal element of society that has been suspicious of "the establishment." To anti-establishment oriented people, organized religion represents one of the biggest threats to their individual personhood. They see the church as a leech on society, concerned mostly with building new structures and collecting love offerings. If such a person is inclined toward Christianity, he may rationalize himself into believing that "you don't have to go to church to be a Christian." Consequently he decides to drop out, read the Bible at home, and watch Robert Schuller on television even though he doesn't care for the Crystal Cathedral.

5. *Disappointment.* Some people come into the Christian life believing they will never again experience problems. They'll have money, good health, and lots of friends in the church. After all, isn't that what "health and wealth" theology promises? When those things don't materialize, they fall away from the church in disillusionment.

Sociological Causes

1. *Poor relationship building.* The focus of the majority of the material in this book has concentrated on relationship building. A sense of belonging takes place only when church members are sensitive to relationships. If Christians become either issue oriented, information oriented, or task oriented, then the church they attend will inevitably have to deal with a massive problem of inactivity and dropping out. Churches which consistently ignore relationships die a slow, agonizing death.

2. *Lack of need satisfaction.* The failure of the church to meet legitimate needs probably contributes more to members' leaving the congregation and placing membership with some other group of brethren than any other thing. It's common to hear complaints like "you don't have anything for

the teenagers," "we were looking for a church with better nursery facilities," and "there's no place here for single Christians."

3. *Internal conflict*. Nothing drives people away faster than internal church conflict. Ira North said,

> In the early years of my ministry, I believed that it would take 50 years to get over a first class fuss. In my latter years, I have changed my mind. I am not sure a congregation ever really gets over a tragic fuss and split. The animosity is passed from generation to generation and it is like the bird with a broken wing, it never soars high again.[10]

4. *Family pressure*. As noted previously, a person who is converted from a family that primarily adheres to one religion or philosophical orientation will most likely be subjected to heavy family pressure unless the person who is converted happens to be the family's chief opinion maker, in which case the rest of the family will probably follow his example. A high dropout rate is noted among new members whose opinion in the family has low regard.

5. *Social strangulation*. Charles Mylander believes that certain groups have unconsciously developed an automatic cutoff point for receiving and assimilating new members. The cutoff point may be determined by the size of the building, the size of the parking lot, or limitations in program and ministry.[11]

Moral Causes

1. *Breaking away from restraint*. In his interviews with unchurched people, Hale discovered that many people drop out of churches because they thought the congregation's behavioral code was too confining. Some complained because churches made up rules on everything from the use of cosmetics to hair length to which styles of clothing the church deems appropriate attire for worship. They got tired of hear-

ing constant negative harangues about these things and left because the church offered nothing uplifting. Others had determined to drift into hedonism, and they didn't want anyone telling them they shouldn't satisfy their fleshly appetites.[12]

2. *Condemnatory attitudes.* Some have approached Christians for help with serious moral problems, but instead of finding a helping hand, they've received a rebuke, a rebuff, and a cold shoulder. Imagine the frustration of a Christian struggling against homosexual tendencies who longs to find understanding among brethren. Most of us would withdraw from all association with a person like that. Many are, no doubt, driven into gay communities when they really don't want to go, but they go because that's the only place they can find understanding. People with such complex problems often leave us because we lack either the will or the patience to help.

The Evangelistic Process

Perhaps the largest number of dropouts among the newly converted fall away because of deficiencies in the way they were approached evangelistically. Win and Charles Arn note, "When events leading up to a non-Christian's profession of faith occur outside any relationship with people of the local church, no ties are established and the perceived need for involvement in the local church is low."[13]

When the presentation of the gospel takes place through a manipulative monologue, through a one-shot Bible study as the result of a chance meeting, or when a person has little or no exposure to church members prior to baptism, dropping out is likely to occur.

Prevention

The oft-repeated adage, "An ounce of prevention is worth a pound of cure," surely applies to the dropout problem. We'll never completely close the back door. The parable of the sower warns of those who have "rocky ground" hearts and will be unable to endure the pressures of hostility. There will also be those who have "thorny ground" hearts, who can't resist the delights of this world (Matthew 13:20-22). But what really hurts is losing "good soil" hearts through our own insensitivity. Some attention to preventive medicine can perceptibly reduce the dropout rate.[14] Here are some practical suggestions.

1. *Build healthy relationships before and after conversion.* Win and Charles Arn insist that disciple-making strategy should involve introducing potential disciples to church members prior to conversion and increasing the network of Christian contacts after conversion. "The more exposure a non-Christian can have to the person of Christ through his people and the church, the more complete his understanding of Christ and his love."[15]

2. *Deal with problems when they first arise.* Dr. John Savage describes the dynamics of the dropout process. It starts with an anxiety-producing event or perhaps even a cluster of such events

> A classic example is the man who was fired from his job. His wife was in a mental hospital for two weeks as a result of the stress. A teenaged daughter was caught on drugs and their son was caught stealing money from the church. Then the couple was asked to no longer be the youth leaders in the church. That's called a cluster of events.[16]

Quite predictably, a person like that feels anger over the way things have turned out. Either the anger may be openly expressed through criticism and complaining, or the person may just withdraw into a shell. The next step is a language change. Personal pronouns in reference to the church are changed—"*we*" and "*us*" to "*they*" and "*them*." The person who feels discontented will stop referring to the local church as "our congregation"; it becomes "that church" or "their church." If the hostility level is deep enough, it becomes "that bunch of hypocrites." There's also a behavior change. Attendance patterns become noticeably affected. Wednesday night and Sunday night attendance are no longer on the discontented person's schedule. Even Sunday morning attendance becomes a hit-or-miss situation. He may stop contributing money altogether. He resigns from any ministry responsibilities he may have held, or maybe he just doesn't show up at committee meetings. If he's assigned to teach a class, he doesn't show up and doesn't bother to get a substitute. The final step is to stop his attendance altogether. Savage claims the dropout will then go into a six-to-eight-week holding pattern, after which he will recommit his time if nobody bothers to check with him to find out what's wrong.

Perceptive Christians must be able to read these signals of discontent. If we deal with the problem in the early stages, quite often the problem can be resolved by simply clarifying misunderstandings and reaffirming our love for the person with the problem. Surely this is what Paul had in mind in Romans 15:1 when he said, "We who are strong ought to bear with the failings of the weak." The longer we put off responding to these problems and the farther a discontented member descends down the dropout track, the more difficult our task of bringing him back is going to be.

3. *Find roles and tasks for everyone who will accept them.* When people feel wanted and needed, their level of satisfaction inevitably runs high. Church growth specialists believe there should be at least sixty roles and tasks for every one hundred members.[17] Often a discontented member will insist, "I don't feel like I fit in." When you hear that complaint, your immediate response should be to help such a member find a significant role or task that conforms to his gift.

4. *Be responsive to legitimate needs.* The church where I serve has a large number of young couples in their twenties. When a church has people in their twenties, it has babies. Recently we became sensitized to the fact that our nursery facilities weren't properly heated and cooled. It's a problem which I could easily ignore because my own children

are all older. I probably don't set foot in the nursery more than once a year. The elders in our congregation realized that our people in their twenties are not only our greatest resource in terms of being the talent pool for ministry, but they are also the ones with significant bridges to the non-Christian world. Without them, evangelism can't take place. We decided we had to do something about the heating and cooling problem in the nursery. To ignore it meant running the danger of creating an anxiety-producing event for our own members, and it also meant killing our chances of attracting others who are in that age group.

Of course, it's essential to be able to know the difference between a legitimate need and a personal whim. We're not to become puppets on somebody else's string, but we're talking about sensitivity. That's the important thing.

5. *Develop new approaches to ministry.* Mylander believes the social strangulation factor can be overcome when we find creative solutions to those needs which are going unmet in the congregation. New groups and classes need to be started. In larger congregations, additional staffing becomes mandatory.[18]

Cure

Although prevention is easier than cure, we aren't totally helpless after a person has gone completely through the dropout track. The passage in James makes it clear that the dropout remains a subject to be sought with the truth. Although there are some special guidelines which govern our stance toward the brother or sister who has been publicly withdrawn from, even that person remains an object of our concern. Paul says, "Do not look on him as an enemy, but warn him as a brother" (2 Thessalonians 3:15). Most dropouts have not been publicly withdrawn from. Whether they should have been disciplined in that manner will have to come under the scope of another study. The fact that they have dropped out from regular participation in the activities of the church and haven't been marked for avoidance suggests that we should treat them just as we would treat any non-Christian whom we are trying to win to Christ. The following suggestions are offered as an attempt to discover effective ways of bringing back a sinner "from the errors of his way" and "saving a soul from death."

1. *Conduct an exit interview.* When it becomes apparent that a brother or sister has decided to drop out, ask for an appointment to discuss his decision. It may or may not be granted, but at least we need to make the effort. In some instances, this last-ditch effort may be just enough to turn the tide back the other way. In those cases where it's not enough, it may serve to open the door for future contact. Sometime ago, I had lunch with a man who had dropped out. In this particular instance, the man had begun worshiping with a denominational group. To my great surprise, I learned in the interview that he had not intellectually bought into the theological orientation of that group. He still believed as he'd always believed. His reasons for leaving us were purely personal. At least, I now knew where the problem lay. I might have made several wrong assumptions about his defection had I not shared lunch with him. Perhaps the time will come when he will reconsider his decision about where to worship. At least he knows the door is still open in the fellowship he left.

2. *Stay in touch.* Even though the dropout no longer chooses to worship with us, we probably have many opportunities to touch his life in the context of daily living. Our paths are likely to cross in stores, at ball games, at the post office, and at various other public places which are frequented by the population in general. The following story is true, with names and some details altered to protect the privacy of the individuals involved. Stan Norton operated a specialty clothing store in a busy shopping mall just outside Chicago. Stan was reared in a Christian home, had attended two Christian colleges, and had done well in several different Bible classes while he was in college. As he prospered in business, however, his spiritual involvement began to lag until he became a dropout. His work was very

demanding. The mall stayed open seven days a week, and he just couldn't keep an eye on things and be active in the church. His wife and children attended regularly, and he even sent generous contributions, but he never attended more than once or twice a year.

When Brett Manchester came to the church where Stan's family attended, Brett decided to make it a point to get acquainted with Stan. Brett figured since both of them were about the same age and both of them had been raised in the same part of Oklahoma, they might have some common interests.

At first when Brett would stop at the store, Stan would be very busy with customers, but they always exchanged friendly greetings, and every time Brett left, Stan would say, "Stop in again, the next time you come this way. Maybe I won't be so busy and we can share a cup of coffee together." One day Stan asked one of his employees to wait on the next customer in line and said to Brett, "Why don't we go see if the coffee's hot down at the coffee shop?" They drank coffee together and talked mostly about Barry Switzer's football team at the University of Oklahoma. Later, Stan invited Brett to lunch. Over lunch, Stan began to tell Brett about some of his problems, his frustrations, his fear that the children might be going in the wrong direction without a Christian father to guide them. He had noticed that his wife's zeal had begun to wane somewhat, and he was afraid his own lack of spirituality had begun to affect her.

Not long after that, Stan was restored to the church. He became active in roles and tasks and became a productive member. Eventually he sold the store and bought a new business in Oklahoma City, where he serves the Lord actively in one of the local churches.

Shortly after his restoration, Stan dropped by the church office one day to visit with Brett. He said, "Brett, I'm glad you kept dropping by the store all those times. Even though I wasn't responding, I knew you hadn't forgotten me." Stay in touch with the dropout. It can bring rich rewards.

3. *Take advantage of social gatherings.* In many communities,

dropouts belong to extended families which include active members of the church. Even though they don't attend regularly, they do show up for weddings, funerals, graduation parties, and other occasions of celebration or sympathy. It pays to spend time with these folks on such occasions. It helps them to know they are still wanted.

4. *Look for opportunities to serve.* Dropouts get sick and enter the hospital. A surprising number of them will list your congregation as their home church when asked to give a church preference. Dropouts lose loved ones. It helps to attend funerals and to go to the funeral home and express your concern. If ever the dropout is going to feel inclined to return to the church, he'll likely give it priority consideration when he's hurting. If you can be available when he's hurting, you may have an opportunity to help him find the way back.

5. *Pray for the dropout.* In one of L. O. Sanderson's hymns, he affirms, "I've never passed beyond the sphere of the providence of God." When you can't do anything else for the dropout, you can pray for him. James assures us, "The prayer of a righteous man has great power in its effects" (James 5:16).

Conclusion

Reducing the attrition rate requires us to be more incorporation conscious from the time we first recognize another person as someone who might be responsive to our influence until the time that person has made it clear that he no longer desires to have any kind of relationship with us. From a church growth point of view, "We can see more lasting results if we begin viewing evangelism and incorporation as two sides of one coin, inter-dependent, both essential for the growth of the church."[19]

Questions for Discussion

1. Evaluate the theory which proposes that "the church can maintain a healthy growth rate if we have more people coming in the front door than we have going out the back door."
2. Why do we often assume that the person who drops out is totally at fault?
3. What causes burnout among Christians?
4. Why do we have difficulty keeping people who come to us with a religious background far different from our own?
5. How can we help people who are uncomfortable with our worship structure?
6. What would you say to a person who says, "I don't think Christianity has the solution to my problems"?
7. How can we learn to recognize discontent?
8. How can we learn to tell the difference between whims and needs?
9. How can we effectively cultivate relationships with dropouts?
10. What would you say in an exit interview?

Endnotes

[1]Flavil R. Yeakley, Jr., *Why Churches Grow,* 3rd. ed. (Broken Arrow, Oklahoma: Christian Communications, Inc., 1979), p. 1.

[2]John S. Savage, "The Apathetic and Bored Church Member," in Win Arn, ed., *The Pastor's Church Growth Handbook* (Pasadena, California: Church Growth Press, 1979), p. 76.

[3]J. Russell Hale, *The Unchurched—Who They Are and Why They Stay Away* (San Francisco: Harper and Row, 1977), p. xi.

[4]*Ibid.,* p. 24.

[5]*Ibid.*

[6]Savage, "The Apathetic and Bored Church Member," pp. 76-77.

[7]Hale, *The Unchurched—Who They Are and Why They Stay Away,* p. 125.

[8]Yeakley, *Why Churches Grow,* p. 25.

[9]*Ibid.,* pp.20-21.

[10]Ira North, *Balance—A Tried and Tested Formula for Church Growth* (Nashville: Gospel Advocate Company, 1983), p. 59.

[11]Charles Mylander, *Secrets for Growing Churches* (San Francisco: Harper and Row, 1979), p. 82.

[12]Hale, *The Unchurched—Who They Are and Why They Stay Away,* pp. 119-125.

[13]Win and Charles Arn, "Closing the Evangelistic Back Door," in *Leadership*, Spring, 1984, pp. 24-31.

[14]The Center for Church Growth, P. O. Box 73362, Houston, Texas, has put together a workshop concentrating on reaching the dropout. The workshop presents an approach to dropouts which has been used successfully in several churches. There's also an emphasis on listening skills, awareness of the reasons Christian drop out, and suggestions for prevention.

[15]Arn and Arn, "Closing the Evangelistic Back Door,"

[16]Phyllis Mather Rice, "An Interview with John Savage," in *Your Church*, July/August, 1983, pp. 6-19.

[17]Arn and Arn, "Closing the Evangelistic Back Door."

[18]Mylander, *Secrets for Growing Churches*, pp. 81-112.

[19]Arn and Arn, "Closing the Evangelistic Back Door."

Index